ENTANGLED NO MORE

WOMEN WHO BROKE FREE FROM TOXIC RELATIONSHIPS BUILDING THEIR OWN EMPIRES

KATIE CAREY – AILISH KEATING
ANGELA HARDERS – BELLA LUNA
DESIREE ANDERSON – DIANE BOVALINO
JESSICA LOUISE BEAL – KAREN COLQUHOUN
KATIE BOCK – KATISCHE HABERFIELD
KRISTINE McPEAK – LAURA MUIRHEAD
LISA PHILLIPS – LOUISE SQUIRES
MINA LOVE – SAM YOUNGZ
SARAH BRIGID BROWN – SOLVEIG BERG
TRACY MAY – VIVIAN SHAPIRO

SOULFUL VALLEY PUBLISHING

Disclaimer

The publisher and the authors are providing this book on an "as is" basis and make no representations or warranties of any kind with respect to the book or its contents. The publisher and the authors disclaim all such representations and warranties of healthcare for a particular purpose. In addition, the publisher and the authors assume no responsibility for errors, inaccuracies, omissions, or any other consistencies herein.

The content of this book is for informational purposes only and is not intended to diagnose, treat, cure, or prevent any condition or disease. You understand that this book is not intended as a substitute for consultation with a licensed practitioner. Please consult with your own physician or healthcare specialist regarding the suggestions and recommendations made in this book. The use of this book implies your acceptance of this disclaimer.

The publisher and the authors make no guarantees concerning the level of success you may experience by following the advice and strategies contained in this book, and you accept the risk that results will differ for each individual. The testimonials and examples provided in this book show exceptional results which may not apply to the average reader and are not intended to represent or guarantee that you will achieve the same or similar results.

This is a work of creative nonfiction. The events portrayed have been done so to the best of each author's memory. While all the stories in this book are true, some names and identifying details have been changed to protect the privacy of the people involved.

Table of Contents

INTRODUCTION

Entangled No More is a compilation of stories from women who share their life experiences of toxic relationships in many different aspects of life. I channeled this title, and it deeply resonated with my own experiences of toxic relationships on numerous levels – not just on the romantic level. Of course, things were different when I was born in the 60's and growing up in the 70's. No one knew what a toxic relationship with anything was back then. Violence was encouraged in society and was often an entertaining pastime for many. Times have changed now, and even if we grew up in those times, we don't have to hold on to those old beliefs or that old paradigm thinking.

In this book, some incredible, successful women share their stories of overcoming abuse and trauma in romantic relationships, parental relationships, sibling relationships, work relationships, friendships, their relationships with money, and, most importantly of all, the toxic relationship with the self.

I have much to share on this topic and have written a separate chapter because I believe it's an important topic to cover and to help women to understand what's going on within them and how they can change the patterns of abuse that they are repeatedly caught up in, resulting in a perpetual cycle of chaos.

These chapters may be triggering as some of the stories will feel like they are yours. I have no doubt that some will deeply resonate with you. I know that each author will be a valuable connection on your journey to healing and growth and leading you back to the essence of who you really are, at a core level and if you use these triggers as activations and for self- awareness you will find these stories impactful.

In the current climate, mental health issues are affecting most of us. Even those who have been in the spiritual and personal development world for years have been rocked by the recent pandemic. Having run a local mental health charity for seven years, I know how our relationships on all levels, and how we show up in them, is at the root of every person's mental health crisis that I have encountered, including my own. How we communicate is the key, and most girls were brought up to be quiet, to behave, to dim their light, to think that sex is dirty, and to be the people pleasers. This still affects young women today around the world, and it is my intention that this book will make a difference for them – the generations of women who come after me and those that will come after them. In a world where we have been made to feel that we are not good enough, too much, or that we don't matter, in so many aspects of life… It's time to change that old paradigm now and educate ourselves, to become the women who are free to live our own lives on our own terms, in a way that we choose and not the way that we are told to or expected to live.

I am 53 now, and I can tell you, it's not too late. I know of 70- to 85-year-olds who have shifted beliefs and patterns that had destroyed their relationships for decades. We have authors in their 70s writing in this book! The younger you are, the easier it should be for you. Don't wait for decades like some of us have had to before we came across this information.

My wish for you is that you live a happy, joyful, successful, on-your-own-terms kind of life. You get to choose how to feel and how to show up for yourself and where and how to create your own life and your own boundaries.

I know that you will enjoy this book and feel deeply connected with these stories. Love, light and blessings to you all, and remember: "You've Gotta Love Yourself!"

Katie Carey
Soulful Valley Publishing

Entangled No More

Poem By: Karen Colquhoun

Entangled No More is the name of the book
It was given to Katie, it wasn't a fluke

It was given to Katie for she was the one
For she was the one that would get the job done

For she was the one who knew what to do
For she was the one who'd find me and you

For she was the one who'd dare us to share,
To be bold and brave, and lay our souls bare

To tell our stories of how we broke free
From the invisible 'forces' we could not see

From the depths of despair, the tears, and the sighs
We have discovered our power and now we rise

It's time to inspire, give messages of hope
To others feeling trapped, unable to cope

Unable to see, to feel, or to think
For those on the edge, or those on the brink

For those who are swimming with the shore in sight
Keep going, keep pushing with all of your might

The world is waiting for you to break free
For you to be you, and me to be me

It's time to open another new door
A time to be 'Entangled No More'

AILISH KEATING

The Struggle Within

B y my very nature, I am a seeker, and if there was a question that summed up my life, it would be "Why?"

I grew up on a farm on a peninsula on the west coast of Ireland, fifth in a family of seven children, physically healthy my whole life and generally strong. As a problem solver, I did not seek out problems, but I did enjoy solving them. This led me to being independent, stubborn, and generally questioning many things.

My younger life did not give me any indicator to my later life. I thought, "I'll go to college, get a job, probably get married around twenty-five to twenty-seven, settle down, have two or three kids, or something like that."

One night after college graduation, a friend's sister asked, "So what would you do if you were doing it all again?"

"I'd be a singer or a dancer." The words flew out of my mouth without a thought, and no one was more surprised by my response than me. Her question had caught me completely unaware; I had no idea that those dreams lived inside me until the words flew out of my mouth.

I had only been on stage a few times before then. When I was around eleven years old, I sang "New York, New York" at the local youth club. We all sang with great gusto and kicked our legs Rockette-style high in the air. Little did I know that New York would be the city that would call me next.

Work was my go-to easy place. On a farm, work never begins and never ends. It is ongoing and all the time, so that was how I learned to work - ongoing and all the time. My college education served me well, and work took me first into consulting, then investment banking.

The windowless commercial office space was hard for me. A couple of badly timed positions in the market resulted in layoffs and severance packages for most of the company.

"Please let me go and give me as much money as you can." I made my simple request to Peggy, the woman was in charge of layoffs, and she did. I used the money to open up a bar and restaurant with a couple of friends in an up-and-coming neighborhood - Williamsburg, Brooklyn. That was my first venture into entrepreneurship, and I loved it! We were successful.

One day I was at the bar chatting to a customer named Xina Lewis. Xina was a five-foot tall Taiwanese-American powerhouse of energy, from LA. We were talking about life in general and our younger selves. "Let me see your palm," she asked. She was known to give people on the spot readings. As she studied my hand she asked, ``How was your childhood?" "I had a pretty happy childhood in general" I responded. "I got along well with my brothers and sisters and my family; it was pretty normal." She looked up at me with her big brown eyes, dropped my hand and in her most non-negotiable tone added, "That's not what your palm says."

I thought about it long and hard at that time, but nothing really popped out for me. Most of my early photos were ones of me being dragged into the photo kicking and screaming so that didn't give me much to go on. I had a couple of minor injuries along the way. I was rescued from trouble by my brothers sometimes, other times captured in their pirate contraptions.

I was often the pit of jokes as I was the youngest and most gullible, but nothing that I thought was particularly scarring. My relationships with my brothers and my father tended to be easier than with my mother and sisters for reasons I still did not completely understand, yet again, nothing too terrible I thought.

Life in New York was generally pretty good. Some things came easy for me, and others were challenging. The most challenging perhaps were intimate relationships. As time passed, I realized a few things. First, I was definitely not going to get married by twenty-seven. Second, it was easy to fall in love again and again. The ongoingness of a relationship was a challenge for me.

Somewhere along the way, I would completely lose myself in the relationship, and then it would fail.

I started my journey of inner connection shortly after opening the bar. I became a yoga instructor, reiki master, and acquired a litany of other qualifications including real estate broker. When I felt my creative energy being drained, I sold the bulk of my share of the business and went into real estate full time. Unbeknownst to me, the first of my big life lessons was about to land about a year later, and I had to prepare for it - becoming a single parent.

The one thing that I feared the most when I was younger was becoming a single parent which was culturally and socially frowned upon. "If ever I get pregnant, I'll move to South America and change my name." I remember repeating this mantra in my head. That wasn't exactly what happened, but I did move to Maine.

Historically, I had a hard time asking for help, and I also had the experience of asking for help in my relationships and not receiving it, repeatedly. The conclusion that I drew from that was, "I guess I am going to have to do it all myself." That conclusion became my experience for most of my time as a single parent. There is only so much relying on friends that you can do and without family living locally.

In an effort to get ahead and establish some financial security, I went back to work outside of the house when my daughter turned two. The hours were long, the pay was low, and the local options were few living in rural Maine. Eventually I found work that suited me and matched my skills. The workplace itself was somewhat accommodating, and I could sometimes bring my daughter to work with me which made it easier as a single parent.

I toyed with the idea of moving back to Ireland, and I started work on a new business idea. The days turned into weeks, and after a couple of years of working on it, the results of my research indicated that I needed either time or money to get it off the ground. I had neither. I was devastated.

Sometimes life seems to take you in reverse. Right after that, I got an involuntary promotion - essentially, take the promotion or leave. The promotion sent me into a 70-80 hour a week summer. I was working more, making less (as I was on salary), and spending less time with my daughter and outside in nature.

The following April, I was in Ireland visiting family. My sister, who had started a company around the same time as me, was having success. Meanwhile, I was struggling. My emotions were compounding internally. I felt like a failure on so many levels. Seemingly overnight, a large lump about the size of a golf ball appeared in my left breast.

I spent the next two weeks doing energy work on it and myself, using tools like Self-Identity-Through-Ho'Oponopono and The Release Technique to let go of the strong emotions that were surfacing, as I knew they were contributing to it. By the end of the month, I had reduced it to the size of a marble, I presumed it would continue to reduce.

It stayed that way until about two years later.

My next effort to get ahead financially was going to undo me again. I had purchased four buildings to renovate with a friend of mine. A long, cold winter, lack of ample cash for renovations, and the pressure to get things done created a lot of internal stress. This time, painting in a cold house over the course of a long weekend in April, the marble started to grow in size fairly rapidly.

"I'll take the summer off to deal with it," I planned. This time it was different though. Less work, energy tools, raw food diets, yoga and supplements did not stop it growing.

That September, I found myself back in New York at a highly recommended integrative Doctor. "The left side of the body deals with lack of support from the feminine - the mother or female," he said. Indicating the emotional cause of my dis-ease.

From there, things just got worse. No matter what I did, the tumor grew. If things were meant to go left, they would go right. If they meant to go up, they would go down. I was traveling to NYC weekly for treatments. Covid arrived, and initially brought some relief from work. By March 2020, Covid brought a complete shutdown of airline traffic to New York. Because of that, I was no longer able to travel there to receive treatments. I spiraled.

Over the next two months the tumor on my breast grew in size while my body shrunk. Friends and neighbors started to gather round, and people started to show up for me, requesting and gently insisting that I go and get checked.

I had not wanted to get chemotherapy. It can be helpful, but it is not without incident or negative impact. I also did not have insurance. I was working two jobs up until Covid came. I was let go from one in March and then the other as my health declined. Going into hospital meant bankruptcy for me with the overwhelming bills – at least, that is what I thought.

I looked really rough. I was down to about 95 lbs, two-thirds of my usual weight. I finally made peace with everything and scheduled my appointments. The day I went in for my assessment was the day I handed it over to Divinity. I was so weak that I needed a wheelchair to go between clinics. They checked me in overnight straight away. This was not due to cancer. My kidney function was low at 19% and my calcium high. They anticipated that I was headed towards a cardiac event sometime in the next 24-48 hours.

From that point on I had started to receive help on so many levels, once I let go of my resistance and let it in. My brother traveled from Indonesia to stay with me and help me recover. Friends and former coworkers prepared meals for us. While I was in hospital, dear friends had my daughter stay with them. A non-profit organization prepared my paperwork so that I received financial aid, and my costs were covered. Kind nurses sang to me at night, and friends visited during the day. All of this was new for me. I felt loved, supported, and seen.

As far as treatments went, chemo would work, then it wouldn't. When the fourth type failed, the oncologist recommended that I move back to Ireland to be near family. I was already 3 months into my 2-6 months to live sentence. She was sure I would not live and did her best to let me know. One day after the grimmest appointment, I decided to go ahead and move. Once I made the decision yet again, all the things that I had viewed as impossible suddenly went easily.

I collected my paperwork to travel which included my oncologist's notes which read "patient appears to be in denial of her condition" and other similar statements. Lucky for me, I did not feel or believe I was going to die. I felt in my heart of hearts I was going to live. When the doctors would read my file to me, it was like they walked in the room with Mrs. Jones's file and not mine, I paid no attention to the predictions. Whether I lived or died was a direct conversation between Divinity and me and no one else. I've seen people live who "should have died" and "die who should have lived." No one knows.

Through all of this, the one thing that still evaded me was the answer to my questions: "Why? Why did I get sick? What caused it?" I believed I needed to understand the underlying mental and emotional cause in order to receive a complete recovery. I also did not want it to happen again. As uncomfortable as it is, I do believe we create our reality. I wanted to understand what I had done, so that I would not end up recreating it at a future point.

In one of the online support groups I was in, two people in particular had experienced a full recovery. They mentioned things like "remember to do the inner work" and "make sure you heal the emotional side." This was the part I found hardest. Where is that seed of discontentment? How do I find it? What is the inner work? Why is it creating havoc for me?

You see, up until then I was considered healthy by conventional standards. I ate primarily a vegetarian diet. I was a yoga teacher. I ran half-marathons. My fastest time I had achieved was just the May before. I had done liver cleanses, colon cleanses, extended fasts, the Wim Hoff Method, climbed mountains, and so much more. I had worked on myself. I had learned to release strong emotions. My palm even said I was going to live a long life! None of it made sense to me.

So yes, I was in denial of my condition as it just did not make sense to me.

Yes, I could have gone and got the lump removed early, and in many ways, I wish I had. Yes, I would recommend it now also. I had healed myself before in my 20's of cervical cancer by changing my diet and doing certain yoga poses. I had also reduced the size of the lump previously. I had thought I could correct the disease in my body again easily. I did eventually, although not without incident.

The next few months would bring me through a stream of doctors and nurses who offered first opinions, second opinions, and third opinions. I heard everything from "you know, this is going to take you out" to "you can recover and have a decent life."

I went to chiropractors, dowsers, kinesiologists, energy healers, and shamans. I had cranial sacral adjustments. I did hypnotherapy, took herbs, removed sugar from my diet and more.

Through the multitudes of hands, eyes, and opinions, one resonated strongly: "in order to recover, your body needs to know that
you will respect its boundaries."

That was new information.

I know that we have an internal guidance system, and our
body wants to be healthy. Our body does its best to maintain ho-
meostasis. So, why did I get sick?

There are four things which I believed contributed to my
dis-ease:

- Stress,
- Lack of Personal Boundaries,
- Rejection of the Feminine, and
- Toxic Environment and Environmental Toxins

I was experiencing high levels of stress in my work life. I
worked in a place filled with never enoughness. There was an un-
ending stream of work with extremely busy periods. The office
was staffed with competitive and not collaborative women. There
was a tendency towards lack of appreciation and lack of recognition for effort. All of this combined with my propensity to work
was not a good combination for my physical or emotional health,
even though I was fit and ate well, etc.

I would not have said that I was stressed. I would have said
that I was busy. But to the body, stress and busyness are the same
thing. If the nervous system does not switch from the sympathetic
to the parasympathetic system each day, the body postpones

eliminating unhealthy cells. Elimination of unhealthy cells such as cancerous cells only happens when the parasympathetic system is activated. When the fight or flight is continually triggered, to the body that means that there is an imminent threat or potential to die. Hence the fight or flight response. It postpones long term health things like eliminating unhealthy cells as it is preparing for an imminent crisis in the expectation that "I might die."

I also had a lack of boundaries. Growing up, I was used to sharing everything with my siblings: clothes, beds, rooms, work. Conversations at the dinner table and in the school were centered around the farm, work, and what other people were doing. As a middle child and the youngest for the first five years of my life, I had come to understand that what other people think must be more correct than me.

At no point in my early life did I ever consider or was I ever encouraged to consider "how do you feel about that?" There was no time for that, and it was not taught in school. I was mostly disconnected from my internal guidance system. If someone wanted something, and I had it, I gave it to them. If there was still work to be done, I made myself responsible for it and the outcomes. I had resistance, not boundaries. I never knew what boundaries were.

So, it was my way in life to look outside of myself to validate myself. I did not know that everything that we need can be sourced within. I had rejected myself internally. I did not know self-acceptance was an option or essential. I only had a tiny sense of self. This is some of what Xina had been picking up on when she looked at my palm, somewhere along the way I had abandoned my inner self.

An intuitive healer once told me, "People who have breast cancer try to breastfeed the world." Shortly after that, the thought came to me: "Does the lack of boundaries impact the cell walls which are also boundaries?" When our body energy systems are under pressure from stress, when we do not have boundaries in place, and when we are rejecting who we are, something's gotta give.

Healthy boundaries mean saying "no" when it does not feel right for you to do something. That can include work, lending money, bailing people out, leaving work as scheduled, not getting drawn into other people's dramas, etc. Healthy boundaries also mean not sticking your nose in or getting involved in other people's problems, presuming you know what is best for others and that you are responsible for them. This extends to family members also. My life was the opposite of healthy boundaries. My motto was "I am just trying to help." I genuinely felt responsible for everything even though I wasn't.

I also rejected the Feminine. Growing up in Ireland in the 70's and 80's, preference was given to the males in the family. Men were served and ate first at the dinner table. Men usually received the farm, and assets of value were transferred to them. Women were generally second in line, expected to marry into wealth and property. The men in my life were kind and generous.

They looked after me well. Through no fault of anyone's, men were favored in the house and women were expected to serve them.

Movies and shows always depict mother-daughter relationships as close, but that was not my experience. Sometimes I got along well with my mother, and other times the relationship was challenging.

My sisters were close to each other and our neighbors' daughters when we were younger. At times, they rejected me and seemed to resent me. Later, I found out that they were sometimes jealous of my ability to get along with the boys and not be bothered by stuff. Sometimes our achievements were pitted against each other. I had no soft place to go.

In every person, there is masculine and feminine. Feminine is honored by passive, flow, experience, and deep connection, while masculine is the active, the pursuit, the action. I spent no time with feminine energy. I was never there. I never slowed down. I did not value it, and I did not even consider it. I out and out rejected it as it had never been rewarded in my life.

Interestingly as it relates to stress, the feminine is associated with the parasympathetic nervous system. The first time I ever really relaxed and sat on my couch was when I got sick. I grew to love my couch. It supported me, it was soft, it was comfortable, it was kind.

Knowing that my condition on the left side was connected to an imbalance of feminine energy, I had to revisit all of this.

My recovery involved embracing my feminine side, savoring the deep soul nourishment that comes from the still silence and soft spaces, radical love and self-acceptance. I needed to release any strong emotions I had related to feminine energy in my life. I worked to repair the mother-wound, and also allowed women and men to support me. I focused on strengthening my relationships with my sisters and offering a whole lot of love and forgiveness for everything. I believe most, not all, are just doing their best, and pure love never hurts anything.

We are taking in programming from when we are in the womb. These patterns and more are picked up on a cellular level as we grow from single cell to adult human. Parents themselves are also wounded children. Some navigate the world with ease and others with struggle. This too is passed down, not by choice, but because they don't know there are other options or are too busy, tired, or hurt to find them. My own mother undoubtedly also suffered emotional imprint issues from her mother as she was born during a time of global turmoil - into World War II. Her mother died when she was 12 undoubtedly impacting her emotionally.

Without realizing it, all of the beliefs that I had taken on board since I was born contributed to my personal disease. Perhaps that happened so that I would become aware of them. Finally, I would let go of these subconscious beliefs and heal myself and any generational trauma. It turns out Xina was right. The pain of being unimportant to myself, the pain of shutting down my inner connection and disconnecting was so great, I had hidden it from my mind.

My body was taking notes, and the lines on my hand had recorded it.

I also believe that environmental issues were a factor for me: smart meters, power supply lines, panel boxes too close to where we sleep, geopathic stress lines under homes from underground streams, and more. These things put pressure on our energetic system. If there is already one or two other conditions going on, these issues are like adding fuel to a fire.

Coming out of all of this, I knew that I could no longer keep the gap between my spiritual life and my work life as two separate things. They were to merge into one place; someplace I could put my desire to serve into action and help bridge the gap that I experienced in trying to understand how this all happened, finding the weak link in the chain.

During my recovery I found Rapid Transformational Therapy particularly helpful to release subconscious blocks. I became a licensed RTT Practitioner and a hypnotherapist. I now understand that the mind and the subconscious mind create the beliefs and the conditions. I understand that lack has an antidote; it is self-love. Self-love allows us to have ease and become free from the tethers of this world. Self-love is a spaciousness that is grace, and you become a self-aware person, the person you intended to be when you were born.

Now when I work with my clients, I help them identify and heal subconscious blocks, grow their business, and grow their life.

This lights me up. It also lights my clients up. They become free from the generational burdens and false imprints that wreak havoc on their life. They become free from both the known and unknown things that plague them. When they do, they heal their pockets, their relationships, and their health. They start to contribute their individual and unique greatness to the world.

Can you imagine what your life would look like if you looked forward to each day when you wake up in the morning and you bounce out of bed, enthusiastic for what the day will bring to you, knowing that you have whatever you need to make it another great day.

Spend time every day asking yourself: "What is it that lights me up? What could I do that I would not need to be paid for?" This is your unique perspective connected to your passion and purpose. If you need help uncovering this and more, I invite you to connect with me at https://ailish.com or follow my newly launched podcast "The Intrepid Soul." Find links to this and other resources at https://ailish.com/resources where you can learn how to leave the past in the past, become more present, move forward with grace, and live a life of wonder, love, and inspiration.

About the Author

Ailish Keating is an intrepid soul and spiritual entrepreneur who is dedicated to helping people leave the past behind, become more present and move forward in life.

Ailish uses the tools of Rapid Transformational Therapy® (RTT) and Hypnotherapy to help people release subconscious blocks so that they can share their talent and bring their gifts into the world.

As a single mother with a cancer diagnosis of only two to six months to live, Ailish had to let go of trying to control things, listen to the universe, and allow it to restructure her life which it did.

Now she is on a mission to create a world where people are fully connected to their souls allowing them to become conscious co-creators and experience the joy, prosperity, and freedom that is available and intended for everyone.

Find her at https://ailish.com or tune in to her weekly podcast, The Intrepid Soul.

ANGELA HARDERS

The Power and Control Wheel of Abuse

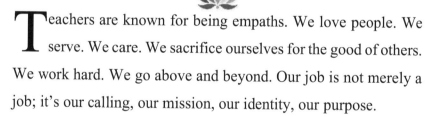

Teachers are known for being empaths. We love people. We serve. We care. We sacrifice ourselves for the good of others. We work hard. We go above and beyond. Our job is not merely a job; it's our calling, our mission, our identity, our purpose.

But there is a reason why almost 50% of new teachers leave the profession within the first five years. Something is deeply wrong.

How can so many people who love children just seemingly give up on them? How can so many people who want to make a difference in the world just walk away? How can so many people who started a career with hope and excitement leave after a few years with critical and cynical desperation and frustration?

I had read this statistic about teachers leaving the profession within the first five years prior to becoming a teacher, so I promised myself that I would not just be another statistic. I was going to make it through the first five years – no matter what! And I did.

I taught for six years before finally calling it quits. I taught Spanish for two years at a high school, English for Speakers of Other Languages (ESOL) for three years at an elementary school after getting my Master's in Bilingual Education and served as the World Language Supervisor for one year at a middle school. I had officially taught every grade from kindergarten through 12th grade, and I was done.

I had taught in schools that had almost the entire student population on Free and Reduced Meals (FARMs), and I had also taught in a school that was located in one of the wealthiest neighborhoods in the area. I taught in a school that was almost entirely African American, one that was an even mix of African American and Hispanic, and one that was more evenly diverse.

There were things that I loved and hated about each of the schools that I worked at. But no matter which school I taught at; every single school had problems. The schools that I worked at in lower income areas had a real problem with not having adequate supplies. One year for Christmas, my parents bought me a box of copy paper and a gift card for Staples because our administration refused to allow teachers to make copies on the copy machines at school. It didn't matter much though because the copy machines were broken more often than they were working.

At the high school, the students didn't have enough textbooks. We barely had enough for a classroom set, and the books were so outdated that they were essentially useless anyway. But again, it didn't matter much because most of the students were not able to read fluently anyway.

I also began to see problems with many of the parents that I encountered. Most of my students had parents that were divorced, absent, abusive, apathetic, controlling, uninvolved, in prison, in other countries, or dead. I have had parents arrive at parent teacher conferences as high as a kite, but at least they showed up. I have had countless parent teacher conferences where the parents never even bothered to come at all. I have seen parents scream and curse at their children while threatening them, "I'll beat your ass when I get you home!" And then I have had parents scream and curse at *me* as their child's teacher for not letting them turn in an assignment 3 months after the deadline.

As an ESOL teacher, my students' parents had often come from other countries, so they were unable to support their students in their learning due to the language barrier. I ended up teaching an English class for the immigrant parents for free before school so that I could teach the parents strategies for supporting their children even though they could not speak the language well.

When I taught in a wealthier area, I had the opposite problem. I had parents that would schedule after-school meetings with me to figure out how their child could have a higher A because a 93% was "not good enough." They put so much pressure on their children to be perfect and have straight A's, and I would watch these excelling students struggle with anxiety and depression.

And I have had students with a 0% whose parents never say anything at all. I wonder... do they know? Do they care?

I have had students lie to me, steal from me, yell at me, curse at me, and threaten me. I have seen students do all these things to other students and staff members as well.

I have seen children experience things that I, as an adult, could never even begin to imagine – the death of an older brother in a gang fight, the deportation of a father, the murder of a best friend. I have had students who spent more time in juvenile detention than in school.

I have waited after school with a crying child because mom or dad forgot to pick her up again.

I have hugged a crying student who lost their teddy bear at recess and another who lost their child at Planned Parenthood.

I have cowered in fear behind locked doors of a classroom when we heard the alarm that there was a bomb in our school building. I have tried to calm terrified children as we hid under our desks because there was an active shooter in the neighborhood. I have texted my family "I love you" because I feared that I might not make it home from school this time.

I have had students that could barely read or write – and they were older than me.

I have had students that were attending school for the first time in the United States because they were refugees fleeing from their hostile home countries. They constantly arrived to school exhausted because the nightmares of their traumas would keep them up at night.

I have witnessed drug deals going down on the playground during recess and had students suspended for having sex in the elementary school bathroom.

I have seen children wear the same clothes day after day. I have kept my closets in my classroom stocked with toothbrushes, toothpaste, deodorant, and a snack for those in need.

I have seen children in the United States – one of the wealthiest countries in the world – arrive at school hungry, tired, depressed, anxious, bullied, mistreated, and abused. And most of the time, we send them home the exact same way. The laundry list of problems that I have seen in the public school is greater than any book could contain.

Nevertheless, I worked hard to try to address the problems as best as I could. However, the problems with public school were much bigger than anything that I could handle on my own. Instead, I found myself hungry, tired, depressed, anxious, bullied, mistreated, and abused.

At the start of my 5th year teaching, I experienced one of the worst abuses that a person can suffer. I was raped by the uncle of one of my former students. I tried my best to go on with my life as though nothing had happened, but as I was setting up my classroom for the start of a new school year, I could not shake this sick feeling in my stomach. I left school during my lunch time and picked up a pregnancy test at a local drug store. I thought, "There's no way that I'm pregnant. I'll just take this test to put my mind at ease, so I can finish getting my classroom ready in peace."

When I got back to school, I walked immediately to the staff bathroom and locked the door behind me. My hands were trembling as I removed the pregnancy test from the plastic packaging. I took a deep breath, peed on the stick, closed my eyes, and prayed. It was positive.

Dear God, how can I be pregnant from a rape?!

You see, up until this point, I was known as "the good Christian." I was the one who committed to not date until I was ready for marriage. I was the one that encouraged students to be abstinent. How could I now also be the one who is pregnant with no boyfriend and no husband? How could I explain my "condition" to my students and colleagues? How could I face my family and church friends?

Against my religious beliefs and convictions, I decided to schedule an appointment for an abortion that Friday morning. My students would be arriving on Monday, and "no one would ever have to know" (well, at least that's what the lady at Planned Parenthood told me). However, the morning of my appointment, I called and cancelled the abortion. I knew that, for some reason,

God chose to give me life out of a situation that I thought would be the death of me. He was giving me beauty out of deep pain. I gave birth to my daughter, Sophia Grace, in the end of March and spent the rest of the school year at home with her – soaking up every bit of the joy that I felt being a mother for the first time.

Shortly after my daughter turned one, I decided to quit teaching. It was becoming increasingly difficult for me to be the kind of teacher that I wanted to be and be the kind of mom that I wanted to be. I simply could not leave the problems of school at school.

My career as a teacher consumed me. I was committed to being the best teacher that I could be, but to be a great teacher took way more hours than I was being paid for and way more hours than I was able to invest now that I was a single mom. I spent my evenings calling parents for students that were struggling and my weekends planning fun and engaging lessons and researching the best teaching strategies. I was barely sleeping or eating. I constantly felt like I wasn't doing enough for my students, and I wasn't doing enough for my own daughter.

I knew I had to stop when I ended up having a panic attack at school, and an ambulance came to take me to the emergency room because I thought I was having a heart attack. The doctor told me that he sees many teachers with anxiety and heart issues resulting from the stress of the job. Who knew that a career that I once loved could possibly kill me?

As a single mother, I knew that I had to prioritize my own mental and physical health for my child, so I said, "Good-bye!" to the classroom and took a job making $12 an hour as a nanny in Georgia, so I could spend the whole day with my one-year-old daughter. Best. Decision. Ever!

I was so thankful for the opportunity to be with my little girl as she was growing up. I began to focus all my time and energy into being the best mom that I could be. I learned about attachment parenting and eventually started practicing gentle parenting as she started to get older (in fact, the first book that I published[1] was about my research and my journey to gentle parenting as a Christian).

Shortly after my daughter turned three, I got married to a lifelong friend that I had met at an orphanage on one of my church's mission trips to Guatemala. My daughter and I moved back to Maryland to be with him, and I decided to get a job in the school system again. I wanted to still be able to make a difference for kids, but I did *not* want to return to the stress of the classroom, so I took a job as a secretary for the main office at the same high school that I graduated from. I was able to catch a glimpse of the many things that happen "behind the scenes" at a public school because I worked closely with the administrators. I was quite

---

[1] Harders, Angela. *Gospel-Based Parenting: A Biblical Study on Discipline and Discipling.* 2019. Available for purchase on Amazon or at www.peaceful-worldschoolers.com/Gospel-Based-Parenting

content to still be able to connect with children but without having to "take work home" like I did when I was a teacher. I could "leave work at work" and be present with my daughter and my husband when I was home.

After one year, I was promoted to the School Financial Specialist (SFS) position. I was responsible for all the funds related to the school. I wrote all the checks, balanced all the budgets, managed all the grants, helped organize all the field trips and fundraisers, and observed where all the funds went. I began to realize that every single school is a business, and every single student in it is a commodity with a very high price tag attached to every single head. I continued to pull back the layers of corruption within the educational system – both immoral and illegal.

The whole system is toxic – from the top down and the bottom up. It's no wonder that a toxic system eventually produces toxic results in students *and* staff. The problem with our educational system is deeper and more pervasive than anyone could ever imagine because the problem is *not* that the educational system is broken; the problem is that the educational system is doing exactly what it was designed to do.

Compulsory schooling is a relatively new social experiment that began in Massachusetts around 1850. Schools were designed in large part by a man named Horace Mann after he had observed the Prussian system which was used primarily to indoctrinate the youth with the values that benefited the government and often ran contrary to religious or familial values. In the wake of the

Industrial Revolution, Horace Mann saw compulsory schooling as a way to manufacture workers for the factories – workers that would be submissive and subordinate.[2]

In April 1924, H.L. Mencken wrote in *The American Mercury*, the aim of public education is not "to fill the young of the species with knowledge and awaken their intelligence... Nothing could be further from the truth. The aim... is simply to reduce as many individuals as possible to the same safe level, to breed and train a standardized citizenry, to put down dissents and originality. That is its aim in the United States... and that is its aim everywhere else."

American educator, Neil Postman, wrote, "Public education does not serve a public. It *creates* a public. And in creating the right kind of public, the schools contribute toward strengthening the spiritual basis of the American Creed. That is how Jefferson understood it, how Horace Mann understood it, how John Dewey understood it, and in fact, there is no other way to understand it. The question is not, 'Does or doesn't public schooling create a public?' The question is, 'What kind of public does it create?'"

New York City Teacher of the Year and author, John Taylor Gatto, wrote in his best-seller Dumbing Us Down, "The truth

---

[2] While I would love to take you on an in-depth journey through the history of public education, there are others who have already done extensive research on the subject, so rather than add to the brilliant words already spoken and written, I would encourage you to pursue their works. I highly recommend reading The Underground History of American Education by John Taylor Gatto. A free PDF of his book is available on my website: www.peacefulworldschoolers.com/downloads

is that schools don't really teach anything except how to obey orders. This is a great mystery to me because thousands of humane, caring people work in schools as teachers and aides and administrators, but the abstract logic of the institution overwhelms their individual contributions. Although teachers do care and do work very, very hard, the institution is psychopathic – it has no conscience. It rings a bell, and the young man in the middle of writing a poem must close his notebook and move to a different cell where he must memorize that humans and monkeys derive from a common ancestor."

Noam Chomsky succinctly wrote in <u>Manufacturing Consent</u>, "Education is a system of imposed ignorance."

While I began to learn more about the dark history of public school, I also began researching another topic that was impacting my life at the time – abuse. My relationship with my husband grew increasingly abusive shortly after our marriage as many lies started to come to light. I assumed that I was just dealing with "normal newlywed problems," but a dear friend of mine encouraged me to research about toxic relationships. That was when I first learned about the Power and Control Wheel.[3]

---

[3] NCDSV: National Center on Domestic and Sexual Violence. (n.d.). *The Power and Control Wheel of Domestic Violence*. National Center on Domestic and Sexual Violence. Retrieved August 20, 2022, from http://www.ncdsv.org/images/PowerControlwheelNOSHADING.pdf

The Domestic Abuse Intervention Project (DIAP) created the "Power and Control Wheel" to help people understand the overall pattern of abusive and violent behaviors that are used to establish and maintain power and control over another person.

The Power and Control Wheel
Of Domestic Violence

After reading the wheel and seeing its application in my personal life, I began to also see similar patterns of abuse and violence in my professional life as a teacher. Once I began to see the similarities, I couldn't unsee them. I decided to create my own Power and Control Wheel showing the ways that toxic teachers in a toxic system produce toxic behaviors that harm children.

The Power and Control Wheel

For Toxic Teachers

I remember the very first day that I realized that I had power and control as a teacher that I did not have before. The first day of class, I told my students that for homework, they needed to have their parents sign the class syllabus and return it to me the following day. When they returned the next day, I was a bit surprised that they actually did it!

I called my best friend on my lunch break and told her how strange it was for me that my students just did what I said – just because I said it. They did not know me. They did not know why I was asking for a parent signature. They could have totally forged the signatures, and I would have never known. They did not know what I would do with this paper or any of their other homework or classwork assignments (most of which ended up in the trash can). And yet, they did it. They obeyed. They obeyed without question.

There was no other area of my life where I could just tell a stranger to do something and expect them to just do it simply because I said so. But even recognizing that I had some unique power as a teacher that I did not have before, I still assumed that I could and would use that power and control for good. It did not take me long to realize how totally out of control I really was.

Schools were created to subjugate. Is it any wonder that our classes are called "subjects"? They were designed to implement social hierarchy. Is it any wonder that juniors and seniors in high school are called "upper classmen"?

We take children, young, passionate, and curious. We assign them an identification number. We sort them in various levels based on their age. We lock them in a room for 6-8 hours a day. We tell them when they can stand up, sit down, eat, go to the bathroom, and sleep. We assign them various (mostly irrelevant and useless) tasks. We exert power and control. And we expect obedience without question and compliance without resistance.

Abuse cannot exist without power and control. This is precisely why we find power and control at the center of our wheel of abuse. Sometimes, when we are in the midst of an abusive relationship – whether that be with a significant other or a parent or a job – it may be difficult for us to see or identify abuse. Many people say that it is only by removing themselves from a toxic relationship or a toxic environment that they are then able to see the abuse clearly and no longer remain entangled as before.

Survivors of abuse have a unique ability to see and sense abuse from a mile away, and that is exactly what happened to me. I began to see the Power and Control Wheel at play in my home and in my work as a teacher, and I knew that I needed to break free!

With the help of friends and family, I got divorced, left behind the toxic public school system, and began to create a new life for my children and for myself. In November 2021, I wrote and published my 16th book called *Tales of a Toxic Teacher: Exposing the Cycles of Abuse Within Our Schools*. In fact, much of this chapter is adapted from a chapter in my book.

In *Tales of a Toxic Teacher*, we explore the various ways that power and control show up in the school system. I will warn that much of what I share in my book may shock and disturb you. In fact, I hope that it will. I hope that you will be so disturbed and enraged at the abuse that we have not only permitted but ordained that you will be willing to take the necessary actions to save yourselves and your children from toxic teachers and a toxic system. The future of the world depends on it. It depends on *you*.

About the Author

Angela Harders has a Master's of Bilingual Education and is a certified Spanish, ESOL, and Special Education teacher. She is also an international speaker and best-selling author of over 16 books for children and adults. She left the compulsory school classroom in September 2021, and now she helps families to create a life full of faith, freedom, and fun!

She is the founder of Peaceful Worldschoolers and PAX Ministries PMA, a faith-based organization whose mission is to cultivate a peaceful world beginning right in our own hearts and homes.

Angela offers free courses and coaching about gentle parenting, self-directed learning, and Private Membership Associations (PMAs) at her website: www.peacefulworldschoolers.com She also enjoyed serving as the editor for this book compilation. If you or your child have a story that you would like to share with the world, please reach out to her via email:

peacefulworldschooler@gmail.com

You can also connect with Angela here:

- Instagram: www.instagram.com/PeacefulWorldschooler
- Facebook: www.facebook.com/PeacefulWorldschoolers
- YouTube: www.youtube.com/c/PeacefulWorldschoolers
- Twitter: www.twitter.com/ajharders
- Podcast: The Peaceful Worldschooling Podcast.

BELLA LUNA

Self-Love is the Key

Before writing this chapter for you, I had a big decision to make - how real, how authentic, how *vulnerable* was I going to be with you? How much of myself am I willing to expose in these pages? And in that moment, I was reminded of something I say to my clients, "*All of you is welcome here.*". So, at the risk of diminishing my own authority as a Coach, I have decided to give you all of me, I hope it is welcome here…

As I sit here, writing this for you and reflecting on my journey, I realise just how far I've come. Just how many battles I have fought, how many demons I have tamed, and how many storms I have danced through. I realise just how many times I have chosen to show up for myself, to keep going, to do the deep work necessary to love myself and my life.

But I didn't always love myself and my life... In fact, just a decade ago you could have found me drifting with self-doubt running through my veins and my inner critic ruling my life.

My teenage years and early adulthood were fraught with suicidal tendencies, self-harm, and sexual trauma. This left me in darkness; depressed and disenchanted with the world around me. All the magic from my childhood had gone, and I found myself alone and at the bottom of a very deep pit of self-loathing. But after leaving an abusive relationship, I decided to get the ultimate revenge – I was going to live an incredible life.

Little did I know, this would spark a journey of intense self-discovery and healing that led me back to myself. In the depths of the darkness, I found the ultimate gift: self-love. But before I found self-love, I found *him,* and lost myself in return.

'Him'

I was 18 when I met *him.*

We locked eyes across the dancefloor of a steamy North London nightclub. He looked like everything I knew was bad for me. Yet, of course, I ran straight into that fire.

I had just been kicked out of an adolescent psychiatric hospital (another story for another time!), and I was as vulnerable as a person can be. I was ripe for the taking.

Low self-respect – check.

High self-loathing – check.

Program set to self-destruct mode – check.

On reflection, he was just another form of self-harm. Instead of cutting or burning myself, as I had before, I was now finding more creative ways to hurt myself.

For the first couple of months, I chased him around like a lost puppy. Begging for his attention, yearning for his love – I smelled of desperation.

He was moderately interested, but mostly I was just a temporary amusement to him. Until, one day, he decided he was keeping me. It was then the red flags really moved from my periphery and evermore into painful view.

You see, the sneakiest kind of abuse is the stuff that builds gradually, like a frog in a pot of steadily boiling water. You don't realise you're slowly dying.

It started with small things. Small things dressed up as other things, or that were so subtle, I would even gaslight myself into believing their insignificance.

He manipulated my entire Being. First by positive reinforcement of what he approved of, then by outright trashing what he didn't, and punishing me when I broke his 'rules'. I now realise he was moulding me into an unassuming, submissive, and lesser version of myself. And because he never actually hit me square in the face, it was easy to gaslight myself into believing I wasn't being abused. For someone with a low IQ, he sure was smart with *how* he hurt me, making sure to leave no marks, at least not in obvious places.

By the end of the relationship, I had experienced the full spectrum of abuse – physical, emotional, mental, sexual, and financial. He had (almost) complete control over my life and my body – what I wore, where I went, who I went with, and when he could *have* me. He had all the passwords to my email and social media accounts, the pin numbers to my bank cards, and the phone numbers of my loved ones so he could keep tabs on me.

I slowly began to disappear. Parts of myself fell away or hid or buried themselves. But most of me just faded into nothing. It was easier that way – a survival instinct I still sometimes slip into today.

He stole two years of my life from me. But I will be forever grateful for the lessons I learned, the strength I developed, and the part of me that held on. The part of me that knew I was worth more and silently fought until I was able to break free and become entangled no more.

Exploration and Self-Discovery

Although I have never been incarcerated personally, I have often felt as if coming out of an abusive relationship must be similar to being released from prison. Suddenly, you are faced with all these choices and freedoms that had been taken away from you for so long.

I had little sense of what music I enjoyed, what food I liked eating, or even what clothes I would choose when I wasn't afraid of the consequences.

I had forgotten who I was.

I had forgotten that I was an extravert, and naturally I could be quite loud, rambunctious, and provocative. I had been acting the part of a weak, fragile woman for so long that even I had believed the story I was selling!

Overwhelming as it was, this experience was a gift in disguise. With a little perspective, it was through this process of starting over and re-building myself that led me to explore parts of myself, and the world around me, that I never would have if not forced to in this way.

I was so thorough in my quest to know myself that I left no stone unturned. Therefore, it was only a matter of time before I stumbled across the *magic* stone and unearthed all the wonders waiting for me beneath the veil. Everything I discovered about magic, spirituality, and the Universe, I learned from the trees, the flowers, the Earth, the wind, the rain, the Moon, the stars, and, what I now know to be, my Higher Self and connection with the Divine.

There were no books, podcasts, or YouTube channels; no gurus, shamans, or sages; no webinars, masterclasses, or courses. There wasn't this constant noise competing for my attention and trying to make me buy what they were selling. I was free to hear the whispers and wisdom of the Universe straight from Source it-self.

I cultivated my intuition and gained an even deeper sense of Self. This was a particularly powerful tool after my abusive relationship, as I developed a strong sense of discernment, which allowed me to stay in integrity and significantly reduced my susceptibility to gaslighting.

This process of exploration and self-discovery is what led me to know myself so fully, that no one could ever again break my spirit or brainwash me into believing I was worthless. I knew myself in and out, up and down, back to front. I had examined, questioned, and re-built every corner of my Being. I was strong. Stronger than I ever thought possible.

This healing journey of exploration was not a quick fix though, it took time. Many trials and errors, countless mistakes and *faux pas* were made in the ultimate quest to 'find myself.' Although, at the time, I had no idea this was what I was actually doing - imagine the potency if I had embarked on this explorative journey consciously?

The Relief of Being Me

Although I do not wish trauma on anyone, and I continue to do the deep work necessary to work through mine, I do believe that many traumatic experiences can leave gifts in the wake of their tragedy. My abusive relationship seems to have been the catalyst for many gifts that have appeared in my life and shaped me in a positive way. I sprinkle a few of these gifts throughout this chapter, but for now, I'll tell you about one of the early gifts that presented itself to me. This gift showed up when I started university, just 9 months after leaving my abusive relationship (bear in mind that I applied to university in secret, and only as a means to escape my abusive situation).

My research suggested there were 40,000 students in my university town, and a thought occurred to me – someone amongst these 40,000 people would love me for me, but if I wasn't *me* then I would attract people who wouldn't necessarily like the *real* me. This was a relieving and terrifying thought as I was still in the early stages of figuring out who I was. Fortunately, I was feeling brave and went full steam into university life, enjoying my newfound freedom and discovering pieces of myself along the way.

And it worked.

It was at university that I made close friends who really saw me and fully accepted me. This gave me permission to explore who I was - to be wild, loud, and crazy, or to be sad, quiet, or angry. They loved me with all my faces. And finally, I felt like I belonged.

This sense of belonging did wonders for my confidence and self-esteem. These women reflected back parts of me that I had forgotten, parts that I had never seen, and parts that I didn't dare hope I had in me. They showed me my strength, my courage, my worth, my beauty, my intelligence. They showed me, me. And best of all, they allowed me to grow, to change, and to evolve who I was, loving me unconditionally through my many phases.

Being so deeply loved and accepted in your full glory by a community is one of the biggest gifts and certainly supported the journey of self-love I had unknowingly embarked on. You see, humans aren't meant to go through life alone. There are many gifts and experiences that are only made possible by the presence and love of others.

This sense of belonging is now something I love to create within my personal and business communities, where like-hearted women with wild hearts and big dreams can see and witness each other's pain and glory, to reflect back the parts that we are unable to see in ourselves, and to lift each other up when we stumble.

The path of self-love, healing, and personal development can be a lonely one. You inadvertently leave a lot of relationships in the wake of your growth. And that's OK. But it's also important to replace these connections with deeper, more meaningful, and aligned ones that support the person you are becoming.

Belonging can make you feel invincible and give you the courage and conviction to take on things you never even thought possible.

Cervical Screenings and Celibacy

In the UK, the NHS offers a free cervical screening programme for all women aged 25-64 to assess their risk level for cervical cancer. When I was first invited to mine, I didn't bat an eyelid. I was young and still had that feeling of invincibility. That was until I read those words at the top of my results letter - '*High-Grade Pre-Cancerous Cells.*'

Even though it had the word *pre* before it, I couldn't help but fixate on the following word – *cancerous*.

I was scheduled for the standard cervical laser surgery and went about my life pretending not to be worried.

At the time, I was heavily into learning about different healing modalities and was diving deep into the realm of Chakras and the Endocrine system. It was this knowledge that helped me connect the dots between my cervix and my Sacral Chakra, which is related to sexuality and self-worth.

At that moment, so many things clicked into place. I had been abusing myself and my body for so long and had allowed others to do the same. I hadn't shown my body that I cared, I hadn't shown it any respect, and I certainly hadn't been loving myself.

My abusive relationship (and even several men before and after that) had conditioned me into believing I didn't have a say over who got to touch me, to *have* me, and that if a man wanted something from me, who was I to stop him?

It was only then, that it really started to sink in what these beliefs and behaviours had done to me. The physical manifestation they had created in the main part of my body I had been disrespecting for too many years. The body really does keep the score.

But when I was able to remember and re-focus on the *pre* instead of the *cancerous*, I realised this was actually a warning, a gift in disguise. I had time to reverse the effects of my self-neglect. I could save my own life. And the cure - self-love! (After the surgery, of course!).

After this wake-up call, I made a declaration and vow to myself. I put a ring on my wedding finger with my name engraved on it and declared that I was in a relationship with myself. I vowed that I would not let another man touch me until it was a wholehearted, 100% consensual, and resounding 'YES.'

Self-Love

During what turned out to be an 18-month period of conscious celibacy, I learned so much about myself, developed a solid foundation of self-worth, and deepened my relationship with the most important person in my life – myself!

I knew I had reached a strong foundation of self-love once I started saying 'no' to things that made me feel uncomfortable, or simply because I didn't want to. Once I started resting more without feeling guilty about it. Once I listened to myself and honoured my own needs. Once I stopped seeking others' approval and started seeking my own. Once I stopped waiting until my pain was unbearable before I addressed it. Once I stopped looking externally for answers and began looking internally. Once I chose quality over quantity. Once I stopped making myself small, took up space, and developed strong boundaries. Once I acknowledged my strengths and began to celebrate myself. Once I gave myself permission to be imperfect and make mistakes. Once I stopped settling for less and started creating a better life for myself. Once I stopped waiting for someone else to *fix* me, and I rescued my own damn self!

But this wasn't an overnight cure to my broken spirit and self-worth issues. I now know that self-love is a continual journey and not a final destination where you can then kick back and stop trying. I use these for guidance, to know if I'm on track, or if I've fallen off the self-love path.

Loving yourself is one of those gifts you didn't know you needed until you received it. It's one of those gifts that keeps on giving. Whether it just brightens the lens through which you see the world around you, fills your life with more meaningful connections and opportunities, or simply frees up some of your precious time that you otherwise spent in self-degradation, you will never *ever* regret learning to love yourself.

Loving yourself really could be the answer to all your prayers.

Reality Check

Before you get rose-tinted glasses about this self-love thing, there's something I need you to understand. True self-love is not flashy Instagram posts of gorgeous, skinny, twenty-something-year-olds in candle-lit bubble baths declaring, "I AM ENOUGH". Self-love is so much more than this, and quite frankly, a lot less sexy!

Self-Love is loving yourself unconditionally and without expectation, especially when you fuck up. It's about knowing your own worth and holding yourself in high regard. Self-love is taking action towards your physical, mental, emotional, and spiritual wellbeing. It's about meeting yourself where you're at and giving yourself what you need, even when you feel like shit.

Self-love isn't easy. In fact, it's messy, contradictory, subjective, nuanced, and requires discernment. Some days loving yourself shows up as making a mistake and not beating yourself up about it, saying 'no' to something that doesn't feel good, or choosing the healthier option for lunch. On other days it looks like crying in bed while bingeing on chocolate and Netflix. Discernment is recognising that one bed and binge day is an act of self-care (particularly if you are prone to feeling guilty for resting), but too many, and it becomes self-sabotage.

I think it is imperative to reiterate that self-love is a *continuous* journey. There is no destination that once you reach you can stop trying. Unfortunately, it doesn't work like that. It's a life-long road with inevitable ups and downs, light and dark, grace and clumsiness.

The biggest act of self-love is being able to show up for yourself through the downs and the darkness, as well as the ups and the light. Show up for yourself when you need yourself most, not just when everything is running smoothly (that would be too easy!).

#TruthBomb!

Now for the most vulnerable thing I will share in this entire chapter, and part of the whole giving-you-all-of-me thing – I hope it's welcome here...

Even as a Self-Love Coach, I am not yet at the end of my journey (and never will be). I still have days when showing up for myself, and loving myself, is a struggle. And as someone who has experienced mental health challenges since an early age (and is *spoiler alert* a human being!), I will likely continue to have some dark days.

The difference is, that before I learned to love myself, I couldn't accept those darker, more damaged parts of me. I would shove them down, keep them small, and not let anyone see them.

Now that I have moved into a place of self-acceptance, I can admit to you that some of these pages have been written at my office desk, overlooking my glorious garden, wearing fabulous clothes and fully in my power.

But, (and here comes the vulnerability...) some of these words also flowed as I wrote from my bed, in my tear-stained pyjamas, with messy hair, because I didn't have the energy to get up that day. Yet I still made an effort to meet my basic needs (food, water, shower, etc.), to remove any pressure to do *more*, and to not judge myself for it. It may not seem much, but even these small things didn't happen when I was stuck in self-loathing.

This is typical in the life of someone with mental health challenges – some days, I celebrate slamming up a boundary, knocking back the inner critic, and smashing out another coaching session. While other days, I'm celebrating myself for simply putting on underwear and cancelling my plans!

On these latter days, the days when it's harder to show up for yourself, these are the days that count. Loving and accepting yourself (free of judgement) when you can't even get out of bed, is the true test.

Believe it or not, I had been on this self-love journey for a number of years before I even realised how powerful it truly was, and just how significant it would be in moving forward with my business and dream of making a difference in the world.

The Missing Link

I started my own business as a way of building that incredible life I promised myself after my abusive relationship. To turn something ugly into something beautiful, to create more freedom for myself, to share some of the hard-won lessons I had learned, and to contribute to building a better world.

After I had been in business for a couple of years, I was feeling a lack of substance within my offerings. I really wanted to create a client journey that was powerful, profound, and tailored towards their needs, not just what I wanted to deliver.

So, I turned to the powers that be, the Universe, the Gods, my Higher Self, and I asked them what was missing in my offerings. What exactly did my clients need to begin their journey towards creating a better life for themselves?

The answer was clear and resounding: "SELF-LOVE."

My reaction was just as clear and resounding, but it was a "HELLLL NOOOOOOOO!." I was immediately in resistance. My eyes were rolling, and I was not impressed with *their* answer. But whenever I receive messages from the Universe, particularly ones this clear, I like to give them proper consideration, so I took to my meditation corner and sat with it.

Given how intense my initial 'NO' was, it really didn't take long for it to turn into an even more powerful 'YES!'

During my meditation, I was taken on a journey in my mind. A flashback experience, showing me how self-love had been an integral part of my path and had created the conditions that allowed everything else to fall into place.

My Being was filled with a knowing that this was the message, the gift, the legacy I wanted to leave behind, in my business *and* in my life. If I could support just a handful of people on their journey towards loving and accepting themselves, then my mission would be complete, my Soul satisfied, and my heart filled.

I have to be honest with you, this self-love thing is not for the faint-hearted, and a good chunk of it will be taken up with falling off, and getting back on, the self-love path. You will come up against friends, family, strangers, systems, and more, that will try to beat you back into submission, insisting you fall back in line with the status quo of shame and self-loathing.

So, if you really want to rebel against the system and get revenge on everything that tried to beat you down and keep you small, join the revolution and fight back by loving yourself fiercely.

Your True Purpose

Like so many others, I have fallen down the rabbit hole of wondering what my purpose was, forever waiting for my Hogwarts letter. Falling for the myth that my purpose was something tangible (like my job) or something super-human (like saving the planet). But after this journey of trauma and triumph, I passionately believe our purpose is to live a human experience. To feel the full range of emotions that come with it, and to then return to a place of deep unconditional love and remembrance of the Divine. To grieve so deeply you feel like you might die, and to laugh so hard, you pee your pants. To scream and cry until your voice goes hoarse, and to make sweet love under the stars. To love yourself through all your mistakes and shortcomings. To explore yourself, and this world, so that you know yourself deeply, accept yourself wholly, and love yourself unconditionally.

So, in a world that is hell-bent on putting you down, seeing you fail, and profiting from your own self-loathing, it's time to embrace what being human is truly about. It's time to reclaim and revolutionise the most important relationship you have – the one with yourself!

I truly believe that self-love is the key to unlocking all the juicy goodness that life has to offer. Self-love is the key to unlocking your purpose, power, and potential. And if, like so many, you are unsure where to start, you can use my K.A.L.M pillars to guide you - Know yourself - Accept yourself - Love yourself - Master yourself. These are the stepping stones I took on my journey and the milestones I use for my clients.

First and foremost, you need to get to know yourself – inside and out. Only then can you be certain of who you truly are. Once you have established a deep sense of Self, you will no longer be able to hide from who you are and will naturally start attracting more authentic relationships and opportunities. These meaningful connections, and strong sense of Self, will support you in accepting yourself fully, especially the parts you deem as dark or unlovable. Only when you have learned to fully accept yourself, can you learn to fully love yourself. And once you have a deep sense of self-love, it's truly possible to create a life of magic, meaning, and self-mastery.

I know it can feel like a long and hard road, particularly if you're at the very beginning. It's important to first remember that *all of you is welcome here*, and second, that self-love is just a muscle; exercise it regularly, and it will grow stronger. And exercise is just a habit you need to commit to. Immersing yourself in something regularly creates a habit within you – and what better habit to commit to than loving yourself?

About the Author

Bella Luna is a Spiritual Life Coach, Modern Mystic, and Self-Love Advocate with a wild heart and big dreams. Using a grounded approach to spiritual teachings, it's her mission to help people fall in love with themselves and their lives.

After breaking free from an abusive relationship, Bella decided to get the ultimate revenge – to live her best life. It was through this journey of intense exploration and self-discovery, that led Bella to find the ultimate gift: self-love.

Bella believes wholeheartedly that self-love is the key to unlocking your purpose, power, and potential, and she now strives to give this gift back to the world. With her RADICAL Self-Love course, bespoke coaching programme, and voluntary work with domestic violence survivors, Bella helps women to overcome the self-doubt and blocks that are holding them back from loving themselves deeply and stepping into their purpose.

Today, you will find Bella frolicking around her British homelands, or chilling in the mountains of Northern Thailand, creating new ways to support soulful women to live a life of magic,

meaning, and self-mastery. To connect with Bella, please visit:
https://www.bella-luna.org

DESIREE ANDERSON

Riding the Crest of a Wave

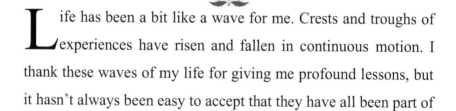

L ife has been a bit like a wave for me. Crests and troughs of experiences have risen and fallen in continuous motion. I thank these waves of my life for giving me profound lessons, but it hasn't always been easy to accept that they have all been part of my unique life's voyage.

Like a pansy shell, I've been tossed and turned in the tides. I've become smoother in parts and scarred in others, but I do feel as if my pain and my blessings have been part of some divine journey, so that I could simply arrive at a view of myself as a precious treasure with a unique message for the world: becoming the best version of yourself so that you can find happiness and success in life, work, and relationships.

I was born in South Africa and spent much of my life in Cape Town near the place where the Atlantic and the Indian Oceans meet. Centuries ago, the Cape was called the Cape of Good Hope and its southerly African tip was used as a refreshment station for weary sailors en route to the East. The ships were laden with precious metals and aromatic spices such as cinnamon and saffron. The crews would brave the stormy seas and the cruel lashings of the waves. Only a few of them would make it into safe harbour.

I can imagine the sailors and adventurers with the sails of their ships unfurled and then finally being able to lay down their anchors in the bay. They would have gazed at the astonishing view of Table Mountain with its banquet of verdant green pastures. This wondrous sight must have been an incredible oasis for their hearts.

My early childhood in South Africa certainly felt like a continuous upheaval with no harbour. One evening when I was five, Mum packed Dad's bags and when I asked what was happening, she sighed and said, "When your Dad gets home, I'm telling him that he is leaving."

And so, Dad left, but not after he held me in his arms whilst I clutched my pink fluffy blanket, and he wrote his telephone number on a piece of paper for my brother and me. It was then that I first discovered the meaning of true tears. They spilled over my face in a waterfall of fear and bewilderment. One too many indiscretions later, Dad had done his time, and we were never a family again. He walked untethered into the night, leaving behind an ocean of shipwrecked dreams. How many of us have had our lives turned upside down by profound events that have shaped us and left us feeling vulnerable and afraid?

A Window for the Soul

We could never quite settle after that. We travelled to other parts of South Africa to try finding a berth for our aching hearts. I reached out to new friends, only to say goodbye when we moved again. I became adept at making deep connections with others for the moments that I shared with them, even though leaving felt very painful.

I learnt from a very young age to find the meaning in the present moment because I realised even then, that it is all we have. One time when we were travelling by train to a new town, we could maybe call home, I watched the patchwork of towns flashing before my eyes like outstretched hands, beckoning and inviting me to a new moment. But they were snatched away as the train whizzed past them.

Only the kaleidoscope memory remained in my memory like shards of glass. A few years later, having moved to a new town, Mum had an operation and wasn't able to look after us for a while. She found a benevolent orphanage which was attached to a Catholic convent who agreed to foster us temporarily. As the eldest child in the orphanage, I was given a sparse little room at the top of the dormitory. The dorm consisted of rows of beds where the young children (including my brother) slept.

One of the nuns was very kind and gave me a skipping rope. I remember trying to master hopping over the rope and struggling to get through hundreds of "Hail Marys" at Mass whilst I distracted my achingly sad heart by looking at the images of Mary on the stained-glass windows.

When Mum recovered, we left the orphanage for good and enjoyed a summer under the purple jacaranda trees nearby our apartment. My brother and I played "hide and seek" under the deep green pine trees and ate ice-creams that always seemed to topple before we finished them. Even though we go through hardships, there are always small moments to remember and cherish.

Freedom At Last

By the age of 12, I'd had many journeys and felt that I'd lived many lifetimes. I was a child with sea-green eyes and blonde-brown hair who was sensitive and deep with a soul that had perhaps witnessed too much pain and sadness. As I stood on the steps of my new boarding school, I could hear the Cape Dutch window shutters tapping slightly in the chilly "Cape Southeaster" breeze. The acres of well-maintained school lawns stretched before my gaze. The weathered oak trees nodded wisely, as if they knew something about becoming a woman that I hadn't experienced yet.

My new school was one of the best in the land, with an enviable reputation for churning out women with academic achievements. One of the school wardens showed me around what was to be my home for the next 5 years. She huffed and puffed as she heaved her sweaty rotund body up the creaky stairs. Her voice had a bored air of authority, and she paused every now and again to wipe the perspiration off her brow.

My sparsely furnished cubicle had a dark grey curtain, a small cupboard, a desk, and a bed. Approximately 82 girls were boarding with me and were to be my new "family." We were all given a very set study routine (twice per day), and we were all expected to reach good grades to make our school and our parents proud.

At mealtimes, the bell clanged loudly throughout the establishment, and we would file into the dining area to eat. After lights out at 9 PM, I would shine my torch in my darkened cubicle, take out my pen to write on a new blank page, and escape into a different world. This was the moment that my love of writing began.

I had a lovely new brother by then, as mum had remarried. She had moved far away and was dealing with her own issues in an abusive relationship, but Dad (who I'd always shared a close bond with) came to visit me every Sunday.

My best friend and I would take extra squash and mathematics tuition just to be able to leave the school grounds. Every three months or so, we would be "let out" to spend a weekend with my Dad and his new partner. He would drop us off at the local disco where we would dance the night away to eighties tunes and temporarily forget the regimented school rules.

I realise now that my schooling helped me have a stable place to live. It enabled me to achieve multiple university degrees, but it left me totally unprepared for later life, relationships, and for being a woman.

One week before I finished my schooling, I bunked out and took a group of girls with me. I was bored and fed up after being confined for so long. I wanted to suck in the air of freedom of choice and claim it as my birthright. So I finally took matters into my own control. I defied the rules that had held me captive. That brief breath of emancipation, tasted on the lips of my 17-year-old self, was my way of telling myself that I could break free of my history and claim the happiness I longed for.

The Grass is Never Greener

Years later, I would buy my first house at age 26 and have a successful career in Human Resources working for leading companies in South Africa. I loved those years which were full of business trips and party nights out. My favourite time of the week was dancing in the summer evenings to the band music at the Cape Town waterfront and looking at the boats moored in the bay and the seals flipping and dipping their tail fins in playful ripples.

The sun would shine high up in the African sky, so proud like a beautiful sunflower, then curtsy mysteriously beyond the harbour's horizon. Gone again was another day. As wondrous as this time was, there was another side to the monetary abundance and fun I was having.

Emotionally, I was in pieces, having had my heart broken badly a few times. Looking back in hindsight, I realise that although I was by all accounts successful, the little girl in me kept looking for a knight in shining armour to love me more than I loved myself. I now reflect often with the luminosity of hindsight that I hadn't spent any time nurturing and healing the frightened little girl that was still inside me.

It was a few heartaches later when I entered into a commitment, but I knew with a sinking feeling deep down that the relationship wouldn't last. Deciding to emigrate was so tough, but my then partner's mother was very ill, and it speeded up my decision when he told me callously, "I'm going with or without you."

In truth, part of me had always wanted to return to the land of my ancestors- England. I longed to continue the legacy of both great-grandfathers that had seen them individually take a life-changing voyage by sea from England to Africa. However, I didn't fully understand then how much courage emigration takes.

When you move countries, you shed everything familiar – all the support systems you have built up disappear, and you are left with yourself. And you cannot run away from yourself.

Having made the decision to go, I said goodbye to my family and my lifelong friends. I packed up all my furniture to be sent on by cargo ship and sold my house. But the hardest thing I had to let go of was my soulmate – my rescue pet dog, Cinnamon, who had walked with me through years of heartache and stood loyally by my side.

On the day that I gave her away to my mom's friend, Cinnamon wagged her blond, bushy tail as if she knew that I was leaving. Her beautiful, brown eyes gazed up at me lovingly, and I stared back at her as if to take a mental picture of this moment that I could hold in my heart forever. Finally, I plucked up the courage to say goodbye.

The next day, we flew to England. I had made the ultimate sacrifice for the sake of the relationship. I'd left behind everything I'd ever known including my HR job for an investment bank. But more importantly, I had lost the certainty of Cinnamon's unconditional love. How many times have we tried to navigate a storm hoping for peace and happiness beyond the horizon?

Working was NOT a Nine-to-Five

The first few years of work in the UK were tough. Whilst my then partner took the car to work, I had to commute for two hours by train to my job. I didn't think to ask why I couldn't take the car. It was chilly and lonely sitting on Clapham Station in the early winter hours. Most days, I bought a coffee and nodded off, only to be startled awake by the train galloping to a stop. When the train finally reached my destination, I walked another thirty minutes to work whilst snow was falling. I felt faceless and anonymous, and wished someone would stop to give me a lift. But of course, they wouldn't have known that I needed help, and so car after car just drove on by.

After that job (which was a contract), I managed to get a permanent job as an HR Manager working for a leading retailer. Helping run the shop, manage large teams, and make sure we hit the sales targets of a few million a week helped me become more practical. Working in retail taught me to inspire people in a more authentic way and be much more hands-on than I had ever been sitting in an office. There was a long working hours' culture and some of the leaders were very dominant and treated their staff badly.

Many of the team members and managers seemed unmotivated but felt powerless to do anything about it. I found all these aspects of work to be very draining and disheartening. I could feel myself getting more burned out through lack of self-care, which wasn't helped by a difficult relationship at home and studying until midnight every evening so as to obtain further qualifications including a Master's Degree in HR.

On my way to my Masters' degree graduation ceremony, there was a huge argument in the car because apparently, I hadn't told my partner the right directions. I remember crying in my graduation gown and wiping the tears away just before the official photographs were taken. I was highly educated and had so much talent, but I was working too hard and being neglected at home.

It was soon after working on a famous automotive manufacturing site and having to quell an aggressive strike that I realised that I wasn't enjoying firing people and doing the part of HR that felt like the old boarding house rules.

My unhappiness in my relationship had swelled like a festering wound inside my heart but my duty made me blindly persevere to try to make the relationship work at all costs. I pushed myself in my job as hard work became my badge of honour.

One thing I loved was my holidays abroad, and by this time, I had travelled to many countries world-wide. I had obtained an Advanced dive qualification and loved submerging myself in turquoise waters. There I could forget my problems and become entranced in a magical world of rainbow parrot and clown fish, happily munching on the stunning orange coral reefs.

In Turkey, while on a holiday, he told me that he would "get rid of me when we went home" because I left the guidebook in a restaurant, and in the Maldives, as I surfaced after an advance dive, I was sworn at for not surfacing quickly enough. I could feel my energy sinking and my health and wellbeing starting to ebb away. I was burnt out by working too hard at work, having to deal with toxic work environments that didn't nurture my caring soul, as well as having to endure a relationship which was breaking my vulnerable heart. Have you ever felt washed out by experiences that didn't attune to your values and depleted your wellbeing?

A Fresh Start

The gravel pathway crunched under my feet as I walked slowly up to the house, I had lived in for ten years. It was in a suburban neighbourhood with a pretty cherry tree still blooming in the late spring. I'd come here for one final time, to collect my things and take them to a flat I'd managed to rent in Surrey.

The court case had been going on for a while, with him wanting to take everything we'd built up since emigrating. I grabbed what I could and left in an undignified way with my pots and pans sticking out of the open car window. I was going to a new place I could call home, where no one would be nasty to me.

When back in my new "home," I finally sank down on the one chair that I had managed to salvage. I had nothing to show for ten years of heartache, hard work, sacrifice, and dutifully paying off the mortgage. It had all been cruelly ripped from me. I had allowed myself to be mistreated by someone I had once loved. As a result, when I finally got the strength to leave, he took much more than his fair share.

But I had chosen my freedom and my health over wealth. It was a bittersweet victory. Sometimes you have to make tough choices to move away from a toxic situation.

Coaching for Self-Awareness

It's been over a decade since making the decision to leave. Looking back on the early days when I first left, I can definitely say that I experienced aching loneliness. It was the type of loneliness where you watch the clock and you wish for someone to speak to you, even a stranger so that you can pass the time in this thing called Life.

I had to build myself back from scratch and excel in my career so that I could find a sense of worth and create abundance again. As a consultant in leading companies, I continued to work too hard, and eventually it took a major toll on my wellbeing. The turning point for me was when I received a telephone call from a friend's husband whilst on my way to work by train to London one morning. Over the loud sound of the rails, I heard my friend's voice on the other end of the line. "Jen is in a coma! She only has a few hours to live."

Whilst this wasn't unexpected due to Jen's serious illness, I shook and trembled with shock on the tube station. Despite this news, I continued my commute to work because I was due to have a particularly difficult meeting with some employees. As I was very highly paid, I felt that I could not let my employer down. During the meeting, I checked my phone, and the worst was confirmed: my friend had died.

This tragic moment was the catalyst for me where I realised that life is short and that I needed to find a career niche that brought me not only prosperity but also peace and happiness. I also wanted to help elevate teams and leaders to get them beyond the self-sabotage that I had created in my own life up until this moment.

Three years after my untangling, I met my lovely partner. He loves me unconditionally and has helped me create abundance again. There have been further trials and tribulations, but we have faced them together. He sees a beauty within me that my own self-esteem had buried under scars from loss and shattered dreams. I respect and appreciate myself as an individual in my own right too, and I have a right to feel valuable as a female entrepreneur and a woman.

Sixteen years after obtaining my Master's degree, I decided to study further at Masters Level to obtain Advanced Coaching qualifications. I felt fairly certain that this was my ultimate career path, and that I would be able to use my training to help creative and ambitious people to be valued for what they do in order to live a life they love.

During the training I had to write a story and tell it to my fellow students. Without realising it, I had written a story about myself:

In a galaxy far away, Twinkle looked out on all the other stars. Hundreds and billions of them all glittering like sequins. Suddenly, there were streaks of light from a meteor hurling across space like a giant wave – hissing, frothing and lurching in the night sky. And then, as quickly as it had appeared, it ebbed and finally burnt out to a point of inky blackness in the horizon.

After Twinkle had stopped shaking, the star began thinking about what it had been. Was it a fallen star or a shooting star? But later, much later, Twinkle realised that it had been both.

How I've Changed Today

I've changed an enormous amount over the last decade in particular. The changes I've made have been intentional so that I could create and experience a better life that is true to my values and nurtures my soul. I've had to accept and take accountability for all the experiences – both good and bad – that I've created and attracted in both my work and home life.

During my training to become an executive coach, I became a lot more self-aware of my blind spots, my vulnerabilities but also my unique gifts and strengths. My voice – and yours – deserves to be heard. We also all deserve fulfilling careers, work-life balance, and to be happy in our relationships with family, friends and partners.

By using advanced techniques such as NLP, together with my leadership expertise, I have been able to help others reframe their lives, remove limiting beliefs, and realign their actions towards success. Health and wellbeing continues to be a focus area for me as I remind myself and my clients that working too hard is self-defeating.

I was so proud to open my own business in 2020. It has already helped many business owners, leaders, and teams. I'm also glad that I have had deep lessons in my life so that I can meet my clients in their journey as real people, and through a mixture of compassion and expertise empower them to be wiser, fulfilled, and motivated in their chosen careers and legacies.

In my personal life, my boundaries have become a lot firmer; I believe kindness to others is very important, but I am also discerning about who I let into my close circle. I know that I've often self-sabotaged because I didn't believe I deserved happiness and wealth. Learning to love and respect myself was harder than I realised, given my past. Many people I encounter (including my clients) have also had a sense of not feeling good enough in some area of their lives, so I know I'm not alone in having had to overcome low self-worth.

I became an Advanced Theta Practitioner in 2021, which has helped me dig deeper on my own limiting beliefs and use this incredible healing modality to help others. As I have continued my own healing journey, I've added Emotional Freedom Technique (tapping) to my skillset to help others reduce their anxiety and stress. I hope that through Crest Coaching and HR, I can help you to see the greatness within you just as I've discovered it within myself. I'm no longer tethered to my own limiting beliefs, but I can now ride the crest of my own unique wave with confidence.

If you are struggling with the next steps on how to move forward in your life or career, find a mentor or a coach to support you. I'm here to help elevate you at:

info@crestcoachingandhr.com

I invite you to download my FREE career eBook on https://crestcoaching.kartra.com/page/5-steps-to-elevate-your-ca-reer-ebook or enrol in my life-changing Career program.

https://crestcoaching.kartra.com/page/elevate-your-career-in-12-weeks

If you're struggling with burnout and limiting beliefs take a look at purchasing my popular Burnout to Brilliance eBook with self-coaching exercises:

https://crestcoaching.kartra.com/page/burnout-to-brilliance

About the Author

Desiree Anderson is an Advanced Coach and owner of Crest Leadership Coaching, formed in 2020 before the pandemic. She holds Master's level qualifications in Coaching and Human Resources and is also an Advanced Theta Healing and an EFT practitioner. She loves combining her intuition and compassion with her international experience to elevate others.

She has overcome a difficult childhood in South Africa and a sabotaging relationship that resulted in her having to completely rebuild her life and abundance from scratch. She has moved beyond burnout by setting healthy boundaries with others, enhancing her self-awareness, and prioritising self-care.

She has built up Crest to help creative and ambitious clients with their life path and careers through training, coaching, and consulting. She helps clients remove self-sabotage and live the life they love, be paid what they are worth, and be valued for what they choose to do. Her work has been featured in many publications both in the UK and internationally.

The UK has been her home since 2000. Most days she walks in the spectacular South Downs near her lovely home in

West Sussex which she shares with her partner Dave. Check out Desiree's website, services, and testimonials at:

https://crestcoachingandhr.com/about/about-us/

Thinking of booking Desiree for a speaking engagement? Browse her press section at:

https://crestcoachingandhr.com/press/

Get your own copy of Desiree's popular Burnout to Brilliance e-book at: https://crestcoaching.kartra.com/page/burnout-to-brilliance

DIANE BOVALINO

Breaking Free from the Chains of Oppression

As humans, the true essence at our core of existence is connection. We desire to connect deeply to other humans at a soul level, and we search for "our tribe" to fit together perfectly like puzzle pieces. It is proven that love and belonging is second to food, water, and safety for humanity. Human connection strengthens the immune system and decreases health risks.

When that connection is broken by people in our life that are controlling, manipulative, and overbearing, then our mind, body, and soul breaks down slowly into pieces that, in time, we can crumble away and find ourselves disconnected. Each time a person in your life attacks you by a controlling or manipulative action when you expect a safe connection, your mind, body, and soul immediately go into a natural state of fight or flight response.

As a human being, we desire a love-based connection in a safe environment. When your mind, body, and soul experiences a fight or flight response, it feels that it is being threatened internally and externally. The natural fight or flight response kicks in, which is an automatic physiological reaction to an event that is perceived as stressful or frightening. This is a perception of a direct threat against your life that then activates the sympathetic nervous system and triggers an acute stress response that prepares your body to fight or flee. In response to this acute stress, the body's sympathetic nervous system is activated by releasing hormones. The hormones released are stimulated from the adrenal glands which trigger the release of adrenaline and cortisol also known as Epinephrine.

Dr. Olga Calof shares in Providence Medicine an article on long-term stress and your health dated September 24, 2021, that these hormones were helpful when humans lived in caves; those with the best fight or flight responses were able to fend off predators and survive to pass on their genes. When released, rapid stress hormones feed every cell in the body, which, in turn, fuel the brain and muscles to increase alertness, concentration, and strength. They increase heart rate and blood pressure for the rapid response needed to free you from danger. After you've dealt with the short-term stress, these hormones leave as quickly as they came, and we return to our normal state. But in some cases, these hormones do not subside and hang around much longer than necessary. Our bodies and minds do not have time to recover.

Statistically, we spend 50% of our waking hours at work in any given day, which means the relationships and the environment we work in is very important to our mind, body, and soul. We all should work in a safe environment. Everyone should be allowed to express themselves, give their opinion, and be treated with respect.

Our profession/career also defines who we are in so many ways. It is the "I am," the center of our being. Our position at work is a defining detail of who we are and a topic of conversation we bring up frequently. If you find yourself in a toxic relationship at work, especially if you find you are reporting to an individual who is controlling, manipulative and domineering, it will most certainly prove to not be healthy for your mind, body, soul, and your energy field.

Let's face it, our parents are dreaming about what we will be before we are conceived. They start to wonder if we are going to be a doctor, lawyer, stockbroker, or the next president. They begin this chatter in their head as they watch their child crawling on the floor, then they share their thoughts with the immediate family, and before you know it, discussions continue in the neighborhood.

At a young age, our parents and teachers begin to shape us with the question: "What do you want to be when you grow up?"

Our parents also are out shopping for toys and books to purchase with the intention of pointing us towards interests that will sculpt our future career.

My story begins here about how I went from being a successful manager one day working in a safe environment and how it quickly changed when the company went through a reorganization.

I was performing well in a management position for over a decade on my way to the next level when another reorganization occurred at the company I was working with. I enjoyed my position as a manager and working with the staff daily. Life was about to change, as I was reassigned to a new female director. It had been over six years since I had to report to a woman. I felt that nervous reaction at the visceral level in my body. My stomach immediately sank, then I got a lump in my throat, and I couldn't speak. The throat chakra was totally blocked. At this level, I find female directors much more difficult to get along with, as they are usually micro-managers, checking in on every detail of your day, not allowing you to be a decision maker, and they find report templates as one of their favorite subject lines in a meeting.

I told myself to have positive thoughts and to march on with high hopes. I was going to hope that my gut instinct was incorrect, and this new director would bring along new opportunities.

I went through an introduction period of six months. I learned her style, and it seemed like she provided a safe environment. Occasionally, she would pop in my cubicle to say "hello" a few days a week which none of my other directors ever did. I remember thinking, "She is performing Management by Walking Around (MBWA)." I studied this style of management while I was getting my Master of Science in Business and Public Management degree at the State University of New York at Polytechnic Institute.

She tried to disguise her frequent visits to my cubicle as an opportunity to connect and communicate instead they were really check-in touchpoints to keep an eye on what I was working on for my branch by saying, "Good Morning! How are you today?" She would often tell me, "I really care about you," but I couldn't help but think, "You are checking in on me. You don't *really* care how I am."

One day, I had to leave the office at the last minute for a personal appointment, so I signed out of the office without her approval. The next day, she called me into her office to find out why I didn't report in before leaving the office early the day before to let her know. I explained that I had a last-minute medical appointment, and I was running late. I put my leave slip in, and in the past, that has always been adequate with my other directors. I was placed on alert to not do that again. That was the first red flag and official alert of control starting in this relationship.

Time went by and more and more incidents occurred that were controlling, manipulative, and abusive that created a toxic work environment. One day, I was called into a meeting room (not to her office) to meet alone with her. She was shaking with fury and put a document in front of me and told me to read it. She fumed, "Would you like to explain yourself regarding the incident that took place here yesterday afternoon?"

I felt like I was being placed on a firing squad, and my life was at stake. I had one chance to save my life by "explaining myself correctly" about this written document which was her perception of what took place according to a staff member that reported to me.

While her body shook physically with anger, she demanded vocally that "I am to not talk about this ever again. She shouted, I am in charge, I am the director, and you are not to ask any questions. Do you understand what I'm saying to you?" I nodded yes as she dismissed me from the meeting room as an insignificant subordinate. I deserved none of her time. I was to understand that she was in charge, and I was to not fight that control.

I walked out of the room and thought, "I can't believe I am reporting to this woman! She is a control freak. What kind of management style is this?" It was very interesting that she couldn't talk to me like this in her office. She had to use a meeting room. "What psychological reason is she manoeuvring today?" I thought. As my mind raced, a million ideas came at once from the intensity of fear, anxiety, and abuse I was just placed under in that prison cell.

Once, I was reprimanded verbally for the staff not taking care of an area that was not our responsibility. In her degrading demeanor, she continued her bully tactics with a demanding list of actions for me to take immediately, and there was no two-way communication, as this was a dictator relationship.

As the incidents and abuse continued, my anxiety increased dramatically, and depression set in. I began to see a counselor at the Employee Assistance Program (EAP). The counselor began to talk to me about filing for disability through my job. The stress was high due to working for the controlling director. The anxiety and depression were still present even on medication, and she was concerned for me as a breast cancer survivor. The migraines had started, and my doctor was extremely concerned as they couldn't get them under control with the migraine medication that they had started.

While researching aggressive migraines, I did undergo a head Magnetic Resonance Imaging (MRI) to rule out cancer. That was nerve racking. As a breast cancer survivor, I have an evasion of medical imaging tests. My doctor kept discussing with me to get out of management at a minimum as then I could get away from her. My doctor understood that I wasn't ready or willing to file for disability to get away from the director because then the abuser would win, and my life would be forever changed.

The migraines were so debilitating that I began to spend my time when I was not at work in my bedroom in the dark. I would have days that I was nauseous, experiencing blurred vision. My head would pound, and I spent months in my bedroom with my two dogs by my side. It was amazing that my precious dogs would take turns on which one would sit on my lap if I was sitting up to avoid the nausea from taking over.

I finally got a regimen of medication to reduce the migraines from daily to four days a week, and I was experiencing side effects from the medication. Still, I could no longer exist in this world of abuse and toxicity as my mind, body, and soul was crumbling, breaking into pieces, and I was about to evaporate from my core, as I did not exist in this world and what was living remained in shock in a constant state of flight or fight.

When an individual is under a long period of chronic stress as I was working for this conceited director then you will begin to have long-term effects as I was experiencing anxiety, depression, and now debilitating migraines.

In the article on Long-Term Effects of Chronic Stress on Body and Mind written by Suzanne Kane on May 1, 2016, in Psych Central, it highlights the following when stress is sustained over a long period, such as remaining in a difficult marriage or working for an intolerable boss; the result is memory impairment caused by inflammation and the immune system. Prolonged stress leads to memory loss.

It also shares information on chronic stress and how it promotes the spread of cancer through the lymphatic system. Research performed by Australian scientists published in Nature Communications finds that stress hormones ramp up the lymphatic system, acting as a fertilizer to promote the spread of cancer in mice. According to the researchers, chronic stress both increases the number of lymphatic vessels draining from a tumor and increases the flow in existing vessels.

Depression, anxiety, digestive, and sleep problems may result from long-term stress. The list of problems associated with or believed to be caused by chronic stress continues to grow as researchers delve more into the effects of prolonged stress. In addition to an increased risk for heart attack, stroke, weight gain, chronic fatigue syndrome, cancer, quicker aging and personality changes, long-term stress may also induce or exacerbate depression and anxiety-related disorders, as well as digestive and sleep problems.

Stress is considered one of the most common triggers for headaches, both tension headaches and migraines. I have always been a highly sensitive individual, and in time, I learned that I am an empath. I found energy healing right when chemotherapy was over, and I just started my hormonal treatments. I was depressed as it was time to learn how to live in this new body with fake breasts, scars on my body, a wig, and a major fear that my cancer would return. Counseling wasn't helping, so I found my way to energy healing. Reiki helped to heal the fear of cancer returning. The depression lifted, and I started to like my new body.

I became a Reiki Master, and this helped me deal with the struggles of the toxic relationship I was suffering at work. I would start Reiki flowing in the shower when the water flowed on me to get the energy flowing through me to balance my energy system first and foremost as energetically, I was about to be placed in an extremely toxic environment. I would place Reiki on my desk, pens, on myself throughout the day, and every morning before I went into the office, I would meditate with the Reiki principles. After I met with the director, I would perform the dry bathing technique named, Kenyoku to remove the negative energy I just picked up from being in the room with her.

After working with Reiki, I learned the healing benefits of crystals and absolutely fell in love with them and became a crystal healer. I brought a bag of crystals into the office with me and carried them with me from meeting room to meeting room. They supported the environment and, most importantly, my mind, body, and soul. I placed a few larger crystals on my desk to clear away negative energy when I was actively in the workspace. I would charge the crystals with Reiki first for an added benefit of healing power. I also wore bracelets and necklaces made of crystal arrangements to support me.

Essential oils came into my life during this time specifically as I was intensely struggling. I found organic oil blends that helped me with my anxiety and stress that dramatically eased my tension while I was at work. I started working with Young Living Essential Oils and became an Independent Distributor. Stress Away and Valor, became my go to blended oils from Young Living, that I use for stress and anxiety. As I learned more about essential oils, I came across an oil that also helped me specifically when I have migraines, it is called Young Living M-Grain Essential Oil.

I studied another energy healing system called Ama-Deus healing which has many special symbols, and it is all based on love. I became a certified Level 2 Ama-Deus Practitioner. I ended up using many different symbols from this system in the toxic environment I was working in to protect myself. The universe led me to this beautiful energy healing system so I could use it specifically to feel love in a place that was threatening to my core. The healing system has a symbol called the emergency symbol which can also be used to lift depression, and I used that with an individual at my work who till this day says it saved her life, because it lifted her out of her depression in such a remarkable way.

I rebuilt the "I am" center, my solar plexus, through Yoga, Reiki, and meditation. I earned my 200-hour Yoga Certification which healed the "I am" center that was in pieces after this trauma. The work I did on the mat with the Asanas and the deep study on the seven-chakra system (specifically my seven spinning wheels of energy) assisted in healing this trauma.

I used Reiki, specifically with mantras, for the solar plexus to seal and strengthen the "I am" center back to its core. I wrote meditations on self-confidence for the solar plexus and the "I am" center to heal. I played them again and again while I laid on my mat in savasana. I performed self-reiki on myself focusing on the head, eyes, and solar plexus. I knew that the tools I have were going to heal the trauma I experienced from the past toxic work environment, and I was going to forge ahead to help another woman in this world who has experienced the same trauma as I.

I opened my business, Lotus Soul Healing Arts, shortly after I left this turbulent work environment. When I work with clients at Lotus Soul Healing Arts, I listen in to truly understand "why" they are at my door of Lotus Soul Healing Arts for healing. As a healer, I must first listen to the client to understand their needs. Then, I focus on the key services and/or classes, which will assist them on their healing journey. It is their choice to decide which specific set of services or classes they want to start with on their path as I am their Health Coach on this journey. It is their health journey and I explain that they can see me as their guide, coach, healer, or teacher with them on this path. One very important element for healing is for the client to acknowledge the progress they are gaining along the way on their healing journey and that they realize the benefits from the services being offered. As the body has the capacity to heal itself, it just needs all "parts" on board to get the job done. The reason is the individual needs to understand their own body in the capacity of mind, body, and soul for it to heal at the cellular level. Once they can connect through the healing services being offered to their body, then the healing at all levels will begin. I am here as a Light Worker, which is to assist the client with his/her healing journey back to finding their true authentic self.

Spirit has already sent women to me who are suffering by reporting to domineering female bosses. Spirit led me to find this book to share my story to find more women who are ready to break free from the chains of oppression as I did and stop their suffering.

I broke free from the chains of oppression… and you can too.

About the Author

Diane Bovalino is an accomplished and certified energy healer, yogi, and spiritual coach who found her way back to health after being diagnosed with breast cancer. As a now 15-year survivor, Diane, with a kind and empathic heart, allows her clients to express their needs and offers specialized techniques to heal their mind, body and soul.

Diane is the owner of Lotus Soul Healing Arts, LLC. It is an energy healing art center that is focused on assisting the individual on their healing journey. She focuses on working with the individual as their Holistic Spiritual Health Coach. Diane's mission is to help women transform their challenges in life into confidence and clarity so they can feel empowered and heal to live their best life through Reiki, Reflexology, Yoga, Meditation, and Spirituality classes. Diane offers all of her programs - Hybrid style, online and in-person options.

Diane says it is her passion and gift to share her healing modalities to change another life as these modalities have all saved her life. She explains that she is here as a Light Worker, to assist the client on their healing journey back to their authentic self.

Diane suffered in a toxic work relationship working in management that placed her health in crisis; mentally and physically. She suffers to this day from migraines that came into her life from the toxicity of the daily drain, pressure, and manipulation from this relationship. She has been called by spirit to share this story with the world in order to help other women who are suffering in a similar situation.

She also has a podcast with her colleague, called Two Italian Women and The Stories They Tell with .... Erica Martin and Diane Bovalino. The podcast is about Life, Love, Heartache and Redemption.

Diane Bovalino is a Usui/Holy Fire III online, Karuna and Usui/Tibetan Reiki Master, Affiliate Member of The Center of Reiki Training (ICRT), Certified Level 2 Ama-Deus Practitioner, Crystal Healer, 200HR Registered Yoga Teacher and Reflexologist.

To connect with Diane, please visit her website:
https://www.lotussoulhealingarts.com

JESSICA LOUISE BEAL

Through the Cracks:

How a Beacon of Light Emerged

My first memory that I unlocked with Timeline Regression Therapy (TRT) with a private mentor was not an easy one. My mother was 16 or 17 when she had me. My father was 27. My first memory is speaking under the crack of my door while looking for my mother. At times, I was using my floor vent in our mobile home as a toilet. My room stunk, and it was hot. It was the 80's.

My next memory was being outside. A neighbor boy was dry humping me, and my mother caught him. She told me I was having sex, and I must have been about 4 or 5 years old when this happened.

I went on to have a very unsafe feeling and perception of the world. As an adolescent, I developed large breasts before any of the other girls at school. This made me the target of many sexist jokes. I was interested in boys for the most part and was divinely guided through these years. When I was 5 my grandmother Ava Gray had heart surgery. One night she came to stay with us to recover and I remember lying in bed and being so afraid to die or be cut open like grandma. A love came over me and told me I was eternal. That I was Jesus, and I would always be perfectly fine no matter what. I thought to myself hmmm that's weird. And tucked it away for 30 years

My father is a restaurant manager, and my mother is a Registered Nurse (RN) in Labor and Delivery. I am the oldest of three sisters, so I can only describe my childhood as having to grow up quickly. My mother was physically abusive and emotionally unavailable when I was a child. I raised my sisters for the most part: doing laundry, bathing them, and getting them dressed for school. I was horribly self-conscious about how we smelt. I can still remember the smell of cat litter boxes. We were horribly bullied. I was not aware of the level of dis-ease that my parents were in.

My father was an alcoholic and cocaine addict. He was a kind man, but he was never home. I remember very often not having enough money for groceries, Christmas, or birthdays. We always had everything we needed, but my childhood wasn't very nice. We didn't have a lot of happiness from within the family unit as children. We made forts, berries into paint, and went on adventures. We ran wild all over the neighborhood. I didn't have many friends and have sort of always been a loner. I keep just a few close friends. Some I've had 25 years. My mother had an explosive temper and was physically violent at times she fully avoided us I think she was also hurting. I don't remember feeling valued or safe or important as a child. I felt like I was in their way.

Being alone was a normal part of life for me as a child. I craved connection from other soul Empaths. I remember being told you had to work really hard to succeed and I didn't want to work hard. Never, I always wanted to be free and do whatever I wanted – not what others were doing. I wanted to experience being cared for, however I have felt alone for my entire life. I have learned to enjoy it and savor it.

My father's addiction was inflaming my mother's depression, my sister's and I were just an extra mouth to feed in their worlds. I didn't see my parents fight or have sex. But my dad would scream at my mother and was physically abusive to us kids. When my parents divorced, my mother was unable to care for us. Three months later, after my father disappeared in the night to a new state. We were told of the divorce and were sent to live with him and his now third wife. She is awful and hateful. She treated her own children very differently than she treated my sisters and me. To this day, I don't know what that woman's issue was with us girls.

I remember feeling mistreated and devalued. I also suffered tremendous trauma around wealth, wisdom, and religion through this family I reincarnated into to learn through and transmute with. I was always drawn to esoteric wisdom, art, Egyptology, and physics, and two of my grandfathers were freemasons. That side of my family abandoned my mother at a young age, after she told her mom she saw grandpa, and he was turned in on a child support warrant. She was 8 and didn't see her dad again until she was an adult.

His father was also a small-town doctor. My great-grandmother is from Kendal, England. She is still living and is 94 years old now. My mother's mother is highly clairvoyant, and it is through my grandmother's teachings that I was trained in intuitive work. She married a Jewish doctor who was non-practicing and would scream, "I hate my life!" from a $3.4 million mansion with an indoor pool. How the fuck do you get over that? Maybe you never do. But it wounded me. For many years, I was unable to receive abundance and security because of the coding from my childhood conditioning.

This trauma causes me to attract partners who could not love me or see my worth. My first child's father was very abusive and a sex addict we will call him "church" That's his street name for Marijuana dealing. He is a charismatic narcissist from hell. If you see him, run! He had seven children in 2009. My son was the oldest.

Then there was Ramiro who did not even speak English when we met. I debated putting this in my chapter, because I felt that these men didn't deserve the platform. Now I know this may be the only chance I ever have to speak my truth in a safe place. I attracted Ramiro because I had a brown heart. I didn't know what or who I was, and for my daughter's, I will always be sorry for letting this man into our world. To this day, there are family members I can hardly sit in a room with – family members who knew what I was going through this year and did nothing.

This book is dedicated to you. I hope you never have to watch your life crumble while you stand alone. I know I needed to experience these things in order to understand the full power and trajectory of my life's work to free women from enslavement... these tools are what my clients and blessings were going to feel like in polarity. In 2020, I began to release all attachments that no longer served me. Attachments I didn't even know I was clinging to like attachments to junky food, unworthiness, and fear.

I do believe my parents did the best they could, so I will focus this chapter on forgiveness towards my childhood. What happened to me as a child happened to me, and so it's what I chose to do with it that changed my life. I had formed the idea that the world was a dangerous place and that I always needed to be alert. The karma I experienced was a direct correlation to my trauma, and this work has defined the path of my life. Nothing is by chance. We always have a choice to flip it around in any moment or in any space in time.

Every member of my family had a very fixed mindset around wealth and abundance. I could see that my parents were working themselves into a trap in order to have anything, and we were still dirt poor. My dad was never home, and my mom suffered from chronic fatigue and depression. I remember that I found others around me for support, but even as a child, I formed the idea that the world was not safe, that I was alone, and that nobody was coming to save me. I deeply wanted to feel seen and loved, but I suppressed these emotions, because I believed these parts of me were unworthy. In my later years, I would take jobs that involved acts of service, performing, and not realizing that I was following and being guided to my true calling.

When I was about five years old, I remember a game my mother would play called "buddy boy." He was a hand puppet. She would have me lightly tap him, and in return "he" would slap my hand back as hard as he could. I never understood why my mother played this game, but she told me a story later that would give me an idea. My mother told me that when she was a kid and her mother gave birth to her baby brother, she would place pin needles in his feet to make him cry. She admitted this made her feel wanted and loved. Why did she tell me this as a 7- or 8-year-old? I have no idea, but it created a perception in me that adults were jacked up, and I never wanted to become one.

The problem is we all have to become an adult eventually. We have no choice, but the subconscious mind doesn't care. It decides what is safe, and what will cause more harm. I believe we all have this intuition, but it is dampened and blocked by society. In our first seven years of life, the world tells us who we are. "Jesse, you have crazy hair. Jesse you are wild, messy, too loud, too sarcastic, too relaxed, too up tight, too difficult, too much."

I was never just allowed to be me. When I became a mother, I knew I wanted to do better. I doted over my first son. He was always a beautiful child, but I carried traumas around his conception and his life. I attracted masculine energies who also carried a mother wound. I saw these men as in need of deep love and healing, and through my conditioning, I went on to attempt to save them.

I am a healer in every sense of the word, but being a wounded healer is a difficult path. The healer does not heal you; they bring you to the place of healing. This incarnation is equivalent to a military boot camp. Each lesson, each wound, opens us up for the light to enter. Every test sent to break you levels you up. This is the wounded healer, the spiritual warrior. I believe it is also in you, reader. It is my philosophy that the most powerful healers and coaches emerge from trauma. These things are not meant to punish you but to build you and raise you to higher levels of consciousness.

The work that I am doing now has been decades in the making. You see, nobody would have blamed me for being a drug addict. I was almost expecting that of myself. I am different. I now understand the power of my trauma. I understand that it has brought me to this timeline. I am able to now transmute that pain into power that inspires others to speak up about their trauma and make a change within themselves, to rise up above the pain and elevate their light body.

I believe to reach light body activation; we must surrender the stories we are telling ourselves. We have to surrender to how we thought things were going to be and see them for what they truly are. When we become the silent observer of our own pain and suffering, we can then begin to release it back to the quantum and recognize that it is not ours to carry or cling to. Breathwork and meditation were the very first tools I remembered through my awakening. I began to dial in and ask my guides and body for answers to my ailments. I began to send healing to all parts of my body and release blockages for myself. Some days were spent crying in the shower in gratitude. It was there that Light Body Energy Work was downloaded to me and born.

This year I gave birth to an incredible program that helps provide energetic support and real time marketing strategies to organically market your energetically magical and spiritual businesses. It is my greatest gift that no wounded healer is lost in the great awakening and that each one has the support they need regardless of the level of investment they can afford.

I believe that when we get to the root cause, we can begin to integrate that shadow and begin to manifest what we truly want to come forward. Instead of being reactive, we can become proactive. Through witnessing the parts of us that are wounded, using inner child work and coaching.

So how do we reach that place? You have to want to change your life so bad that you will do anything. You have to be open to do the things that scare you because that is what is standing between you and your dream. Just take one small step at a time, even if you can't see the destination.

The actual power comes from moving toward the experience. I did not come to meditation to heal others; I arrived at it to heal myself. Healing and leading others became secondary. I knew I had achieved something powerful and that it was not only meant for me. I knew that what I had unlocked was also going to help others. I once heard a statement from a great yogi that said this, "The earth supports those that support life." That resonates with me. It was clear to me that I needed to release these traumas I was clinging to and let go of attachments that no longer serve me.

I feel so strongly about helping others get activated, discover their real potential and purpose, and craft a life that is fulfilled and filled with freedom however that abundance looks for them. Maybe it's a turtle, maybe it's travel, or buying a home? I want all women to remember and stand in their power, to learn incantations, rituals, and tap back into her divine feminine power. I believe, as we heal, we can extend our arms and reach out to pull others up.

Women stick together. I have made it my soul mission to help as many women as I can in my lifetime step into power and financial stability. There truly is no external recession, because daily light workers, coaches, and mentors are expanding and upleveling! We are the change makers, the free thinkers, the masters of the elevation of consciousness. I want to let you know that what happens to you does not define you. You are a multidimensional being that was born from the earth. You have everything inside you to create the life you want.

Even when it feels like the answer is unclear, you need only call on your guides and meditate to find the answer. If I could leave you with anything in this chapter, it is the ability to tap in and channel for yourself. Any time you are in need of a tool or answer you need only reach out your hand and ask your angels, "Angels, please give me the tools needed for _____. Thank you!" You will feel something placed in your hand, and almost immediately, you will be granted what you seek. The other tool is meditation. You can spend seven years in a forest with monks, or you can take my coursework. Light Body Energy Work is simple, and anyone can practice this work.

Get into a quiet place. Sit up straight to let the energy of the chakras flow at an optimal state. You do not need to understand the details, however nasal breathing is key. Focus on a pattern of 4.7.8. Inhale for 4, hold for 7, exhale continuing to breath only with the nose for 8 seconds. The mouth is for eating, the nose is for breathing. It is in the sound that the energy is charged, and necessary chemicals are also made to regulate our bodies in this state.

The brain works best with a little starvation. When a thought arises, witness it, and let it fall away, focusing back to the breach. The witness is a judgement-free being, all knowing and forgiving. How do you speak to yourself? Would you speak to your best friend this way? If not, then don't say it to or about yourself. Speak highly of yourself. You are the goddess. A daily practice of meditation can help you to take a deeper look at the parts of you that are bringing you the most dis-ease. I also highly recommend intermittent fasting and have 10+ years of experience in plant therapy and essential oils with Young Living Global. Oils were my first energy work.

I highly recommend journaling what comes up and working through it with an experienced mentor, therapist, or guide with whom you resonate. With meditation, we are able to send cellular healing throughout the body. Give yourself some grace. Meditation and mindfulness can take time to master. One of my favorite mentors, Ram Dass, taught me much about spirituality, but the biggest take away was this: the ego is who we think we are, the soul is who we *really* are.

Through meditation, I began to experience brilliant downloads of information and powers that have brought me to this moment today, manifesting my dreams, and teaching esoteric wisdom. I discovered the power of the Incantations I AM – and believe it to be the vibration of all creation. When we manifest, we do not move from a place of I want or I need, but I am. I say do whatever lights you up, and you will forever be free. Your circumstances do not define you, sisters. It's what you make of them. Nobody can take away the data you put in your mind. Push back, quiet your mind, keep showing up. *Namaste*, and be well, friends.

About the Author

Jessica Louise Beal is a certified Meditation Practitioner, Sound Healer, and Sacred Business strategist. In 2019, she began to experience symptoms of a spiritual awakening and found the power to escape a domestic violence and sexual abuse situation.

Through ascension, she began to unravel deep core wounds and generational trauma. She learned to soothe her nervous system and move from fear and scarcity to abundance.

Jessica is the CREATRIX of Light Body Activation, a podcast on Spotify and Anchor, and Quiet Your Mind, a free Meditation circle where she hosts monthly workshops.

Jessica is also a social media strategist to spiritual Entrepreneurs sharing her unique light codes and proven 3 and 5D strategies, guiding others into Monetization. It is her greatest passion to be in deep service to others and help them create freedom through activating their own power and divine medicines. To connect with Jessica, please visit: https://linktr.ee/JessicaBeal

KAREN COLQUHOUN

From Fear to Freedom:

My Journey to a Conscious Life

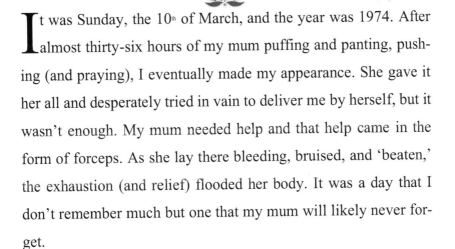

It was Sunday, the 10ᵗʰ of March, and the year was 1974. After almost thirty-six hours of my mum puffing and panting, pushing (and praying), I eventually made my appearance. She gave it her all and desperately tried in vain to deliver me by herself, but it wasn't enough. My mum needed help and that help came in the form of forceps. As she lay there bleeding, bruised, and 'beaten,' the exhaustion (and relief) flooded her body. It was a day that I don't remember much but one that my mum will likely never forget.

Like most of us, I don't recall much about my early days as a newborn baby, but I've been told I was beautiful. I was born with dark brown hair and dark brown eyes that were almost black like my dad's. I had my Nana's short, stubby nose and my mum's rosy, slim lips. I've seen some old photos of me as a baby. I *was* beautiful. In fact, I was perfect, and back then, I KNEW IT!

This 'knowing' of who I was, that I was perfectly imperfect, that I was worthy (of everything), and that I was enough (exactly as I was) is something that we all embody when we are born. Unfortunately, these 'truths' about each and every one of us become distorted over time by the hopes, the dreams, the fears, and the beliefs of our caregivers and teachers, by the standards and expectations of the education system and society as a whole, by our own need for attachment and the desire to meet the needs and wants of those we ultimately choose to become friends or partners.

Re-embodying this deep knowing of the truth, of who we are, of our worth, of our infinite potential is possible for everyone, but it can only be activated and accomplished by ourselves. Nobody else can do it for us!

This is my story of re-discovering my truths and of becoming disentangled from the lies.

Pre-School, age 3 - 4

My long-term memory doesn't always serve me well, but there is a childhood experience that sticks in my mind. It is the same memory that has come to the surface almost every time I have undergone hypnosis to release 'something.' I'm not sure what age I was, but I am sure that it was this event that started me on my journey of creating negative beliefs about myself and developing fears that would cripple me for most of my life. This is my (somewhat vivid) recollection of that day...

It must have been a 'nice' day, or at least it must not have been raining, as I wouldn't have been allowed out if it was. You see, my mum was conditioned to fear the rain, to believe that it 'made you ill.' She often had to walk to and from school not just in the rain, but in the hail and snow too. Mum was born in the 50's. At a time when it was either eat or heat, my mum and her siblings would catch colds and chest infections just like many others.

Another of my mum's beliefs back then would have been that it 'wasn't safe to play outside at such a young age.' but I'm guessing she 'caved in' and let me 'out of her sight' to play round the back. I'm not entirely sure how long my cousin and I were out playing or what we could've been playing with, but at some point, I decided that it was okay to go to the toilet outside. (Not that there was an outside toilet). Unfortunately for me, my cousin thought it was okay to tell my mum

My mum had a really traumatic upbringing and came from a homelife where adverse childhood experiences were a daily occurrence. I won't go into every detail here, but what I will say is that my grandad was strict (likely because his parents were strict), so it was no surprise that my mum would also be strict with me and my siblings. Mum did a great job of teaching us 'right from wrong.' We were well 'trained' to be polite and well-behaved, to obey and follow rules, but that day, I must've forgotten the one about not going to the toilet outside.

When I return to 'that' day, I can sense her disappointment and her anger at what I had done. I can sense her frustration at my innocence and ignorance of the 'dangers' of doing such a thing, in broad daylight, in front of 'everyone'. I can feel my heart pounding in my chest, and the fear trapped in my throat. I feel my bum sting, and I hear the words: "For god's sake, she's only a wean."

At that moment, as my mum fell prey to her big emotions and her need to 'do the right thing,' to teach me that actions have consequences, I tried to make sense of it all. I knew I had done wrong. I knew I had made a mistake. I knew that I had let her down. What I didn't know was that in my search for answers about why my mum had reacted the way she did, I created a story. I created a story and from this story I created beliefs about myself, beliefs that made themselves comfy, right at home, snuggled deep down in my subconscious...

"I am bad."

"I deserve to be punished."

"I am unworthy of my mum's love."

My mum didn't always get it right, but she made sure we were well cared for and looked after to the best of her ability. Whilst my dad worked, she cooked, she cleaned, and she kissed us every night at bedtime. We were bathed daily and always had freshly washed pyjamas to put on afterwards. We always had neatly made beds to climb into. I knew deep down I wasn't bad and that I was worthy of her love. We all were.

1981, age 7

Sore throats, colds, and chest infections were the norm as we grew up. If one of us caught something, it would have been passed around until we'd all had a shot. I must've had more than my fair share of tonsilitis because I have a memory of being in Yorkhill Children's Hospital after having my tonsils and adenoids removed. It wasn't the done thing for parents to stay overnight back then, and even if it was, my mum had my brothers and sister to look after whilst my dad went to work.

Although I now completely understand and accept that it just wasn't true, that old story about not being worthy of my mum's love crept back into my awareness for a split second. It slowly slipped back into my subconscious as I tucked into the ice cream and jelly given to me by the nurse (in an attempt to soothe the red-raw sores at the back of my throat).

I'm sure I had that same story reappear each night my mum left, but it wasn't all bad… right there, in the centre of the ward stood a huge, wooden rocking horse. It was obviously for the children (to lessen the trauma of being away from home), and we were 'allowed' to sit on it. After a while, once the other children had their turn, and I'd mustered up the courage, I stepped up to take mine. I loved it – not just because it was sturdy, (and, therefore, safe) but because I somehow 'accidently' banged the middle finger on my right hand and the unsightly, 'dirty' wart that I had grown to hate, fell off! As I write this now, I can't help but feel that I had begun manifesting, not on purpose, but manifesting all the same!

1985, age 11

Mrs. Greene, a teacher who was both loved and feared in equal measures, was my Primary 7 teacher. She had a younger sister, Miss McGowan, who taught us music. Despite the age gap and slight difference in hair colouring, they looked alike but had completely different personalities. Miss McGowan was soft-spoken and had a gentle energy about her, but her older sister? Not so much. I remember the long nails and the narrowed eyes when Mrs. Greene was angry (not at me, but at those who dared to disobey her). I was very fond of her. She smiled at me often and praised me for all sorts of things, one of which was my handwriting (which I am still complemented on to this day). Mrs. Greene approved of my 'positive attitude to school' and my 'ability to grasp new concepts quickly.' She praised my efforts and often identified me as a role model for others in the class. Rose Greene also filled my heart with joy as she sat at the front of the class on her wooden 'highchair' whilst reading aloud the novel of *her* choice.

Like I said, my long-term memory doesn't always serve me well, but for some reason, I remember a lot about that year. I remember learning about Carrie's War and feeling deeply for the trauma faced by Carrie and her younger brother Nick. I also remember scoring ninety-nine out of one hundred in a spelling competition and being awarded with a pound. It was a well-earned pound note, and it was all mine!

Being a 'good girl' and pleasing my teachers was something that I had mastered; I don't remember getting into trouble at Primary School, but there was one occasion where I absolutely would have, had I been brave enough to face my fears. I couldn't face the fear of disappointing Mrs. Greene, or the hurt or the rejection that I might've felt from the others involved, so I kept my mouth shut.

The toilet event I described above left me with thoughts that eventually became my core beliefs about me and my worth, but it also caused me to develop a fear of disapproval and on a deeper level, a fear of rejection. It was this fear of rejection and attachment to the love and approval of others that would cause me to attract not one, or two, but three toxic relationships. I will visit each of these later, but first I would like to share what happened in my first year at High School.

1986 - 1987, age 12 - 13

I have always loved learning! I pride myself in the knowledge, understanding, and skills that I have accumulated throughout my life. After all, it's through this learning that I have become who I am today. I loved St. John Ogilvie, and I loved St. Leonard's even more.

On my first day of High School, we all gathered in the gym hall waiting anxiously to find out what class we'd be in. There seemed to be hundreds of people, but there couldn't have been that many, as we were split into only 4 classes - 1A, 1B, 1C and 1D. I was placed in 1B. My most significant year at St. Leonard's was my first year, but not because it was a new year or the beginning of my journey to a bright future, but because looking back, this was the year that my life was thrown into turmoil.

French was one of the many subjects that I excelled at. I loved everything about it, and I was thrilled to remain top of the class, despite the illness that knocked me for six. I didn't know I was ill. I didn't feel ill, and I certainly didn't look ill, but something didn't sit right with my P.E. teacher, Mrs. Kearney. The bruises on my arms and legs set alarm bells ringing, and the next thing I knew, I was being escorted from my French lesson to the Headteacher's office. My mum was waiting for me, and without much explanation as to why or what was going on, I was taken once again to Glasgow Royal Infirmary, this time to the Haematology Department.

Somewhere between my teacher raising concerns, my mum speaking to the GP, and me heading to the hospital, it must've been decided that I wasn't 'at risk' and that the only explanation for the bruises could be that I might have leukaemia. I can only imagine the thoughts and feelings running through my mum's head and body. I didn't know for sure because she never said. She put on a brave face like she always did (and still does).

The routine procedure to check for leukaemia was to carry out a lumbar puncture. I was terrified, but I didn't dare resist. I lay there and let them do their job. I was 'a star,' and my reward was a cold can of diet coke. My back was sore, but, boy, did that can of coke taste good!

It turns out that it wasn't leukaemia but a blood disorder called Immune Thrombocytopenic Purpura which is characterised by a decrease in the number of platelets. Platelets help stop bleeding, and a decrease can cause easy bruising, which explained those that randomly appeared on my body.

The plan was for me to be put on steroids. After many months of decreasing the dose and then increasing it again as the platelet levels dropped, I asked if there was anything else they could do. The weight had piled on, and I was losing sight of who I was. I literally didn't recognise myself in the mirror. I knew it was me, but I hated who I'd become.

Much to my delight, there *was* something else they could do. I could have my spleen removed which would mean no more steroids. I agreed to the splenectomy, and despite the odd flu or chest infection, I've managed to remain in good health.

I remember 'going out' with someone whilst on the steroids, but as I grew bigger the fear grew stronger. I ended the 'relationship' and retreated into my shell. I didn't understand my reaction then, but I do now… I felt unworthy of his love and feared the rejection that would 'prove' it.

1989 - 1990, age 15 - 16

The first of my toxic relationships happened at an age when I was vulnerable, naïve, and in no way shape or form, emotionally mature enough to deal with the heartache that I felt at being dumped on the phone for someone else. At some point, after many months of tears and Whitney Houston tracks, I 'recovered' just enough to move on with my life. Well, I say I 'recovered,' but actually I didn't. I just buried the pain. I disconnected from the trauma and created a new belief…

"I'm not enough."

1992 - 2000, age 18 - 26

The second of my toxic relationships lasted 8 years and ended the night I decided that I didn't love him anymore. I was done with the put downs and snide remarks about how good-looking other girls were. I couldn't suffer his Jekyll and Hyde nature anymore. I'd had enough!

I had always put the erratic change in his attitude and behaviour towards me down to the alcohol, but I knew the truth. It wasn't the alcohol, it's who he was, who he learned to be as he watched his father treat his mother in the exact same way.

This relationship was easier to walk away from, but it wasn't easy. I cried for days – not because it wasn't what I wanted, but because I knew he was hurting the way I had been hurting a few years earlier.

2000 - 2011, age 26 - 37

It was this relationship that changed my life in more ways than one. I won't go into detail, but it taught me more about myself than any other. It highlighted the repeating patterns I had made (and was making) in my life, the co-dependency, the need for approval and validation. It also highlighted my search and craving for love from others.

"It's taken me a while, but I now realise that it wasn't love from others that I was looking for, it was love from and for myself!"

I haven't always been a good judge of character, particularly when it comes to the opposite sex. As a teenager and young adult, I was shy and lacked confidence, so when my path crossed with someone good looking and 'nice,' I was instantly attracted to them! I fell hook, line, and sinker especially if they also had nice teeth and a good sense of humour.

"Within each of these relationships, I loved and lost, not always my 'other half' but myself. I lost ME!"

Back then, I didn't ever think about who I was or what I wanted; it was all about them, making them happy and meeting their needs. I had inherited many dysfunctional patterns of behaviour from my mum, my gran, and so on; patterns that until recently, I was completely unaware of. Besides the people pleasing and putting others first, others that have come to the fore include suffering in silence, lacking boundaries, and accepting what was believed to have been fate.

I do believe in fate, and it *was* fate that whilst I lived, laughed, loved, and learned from each of these relationships. They were never meant to last forever. They were meant to help me grow and awaken to the possibility of finding true love. They were meant to help me become aware of who I was, what I wanted, but also what I didn't want or deserve.

27th of March 2008 and 25th of November 2010

These are the dates of when I received my greatest gifts from God, my beautiful children, Ben and Ava. I had always wanted to be a mum and had tried (and failed) for several years. I feared that it was never going to happen, but on returning from a week's holiday to Marmaris in Turkey, I discovered that I was pregnant and that in six months' time I would get to meet the tiny miracle growing inside me.

Ben was everything that I had hoped for and more! He was beautiful, and he was perfectly imperfect – just like me. Life as a first-time mum was tough. My boy was a hungry baby, and I wasn't prepared for the daily night feeds at 1 am and 4 am. The sleep deprivation and the sheer exhaustion could've (and probably should've) put me off having another, but I didn't want Ben growing up an only child. I had siblings, and I couldn't bear the thought of him being 'alone.'

Ava was my second gift from God; she was not only the daughter that I had been praying for but was the one who would become my biggest teacher. I believe Ava has come forth to help me heal and break free from the generational patterns that have unconsciously and unintentionally been passed to me (and her) from our ancestors.

I love them both dearly and I am blessed to be their mum.

3rd of April 2016

I've only just realised, as I sit here typing away on my yellow leather sofa, that it was at this time that my journey of releasing myself from the limiting beliefs and fears that I had inherited (or created myself) had already begun.

My fear of being judged and of the disapproval from others had gone, or rather, had lay dormant, beneath the surface as the knowledge that I had met 'the one' took hold of my mind, body, and soul. I knew this was it. I had 'suffered' enough, and I was ready to apply what I had learned.

We met on Sunday the 3rd of April (which was Ben's due date eight years earlier), and it was love at first sight. As I looked up to Robert walking towards me, I remember thinking, "Omg, I'm going to fall madly in love with him."

Falling in love wasn't unusual for me, but I just knew this time was different. I wasn't just attracted to the way he looked and smelled, or to his teeth and sense of humour. It was deeper than that; it was familiar, as if I had known him all my life.

Robert and I married that same year on the 16th of October, just six months after our first date. He has been a constant source of love and support for me and the dad that Ben and Ava have always needed and deserved. A past life reading revealed that Robert was my husband from a previous life and that he had come forth to be with me in this lifetime, so that I could heal and so that I could fulfil my soul contract. I appreciate that some may think this is absolute nonsense or that it's impossible, but I believe it to be true, and that's all that matters.

"I choose to let go of the opinion of others,

for their opinions are none of my business."

October 2019

I remember a few years back, not quite the day or the date, but I remember the feelings of overwhelm, of sighing, trying, and failing (miserably), of wishing life wasn't so hard. I remember the thought that seemed to appear from nowhere: "*There must be more to life than this!*"

That thought was not from nowhere, and it was not the one that catapulted me into my spiritual 'awakening.' I didn't know it at the time, but I had already started to awaken many years back in 2011 when I asked Ben and Ava's dad to leave. In March that year, I came to my senses and started to see the light. I started to believe that I deserved more and that, one day, I would have more.

20th of March 2020

This date marks the time when the world 'came to a standstill,' but for me it also marks the time in which my awakening really began to gain momentum. It hasn't just been about discovering spirituality and the Law of Attraction or the Universe and other universal laws. It hasn't even just been about understanding and accepting that we are all energy and that we have the potential to be, do, and have whatever we want.

It's been a rollercoaster ride of highs and lows, good days and 'bad,' happiness and sadness. It's been a trip down memory lane and revisiting events that still held an emotional charge within the cells of my body. It's been dark, and it's been heavy, but it's also been light and transformational. It's shed light on what I came here to experience, and it's given me opportunities to heal so that I can help other mums to do the same.

How I began to break free...

- Developing my knowledge, understanding, and ability to use spiritual practices helped me look after my mind, body, and soul. There are many spiritual practices that I have tried but the ones that I believe work for me are: having an attitude of gratitude, journaling, and meditating.

- Becoming self-aware of my thoughts and feelings has also been key for me, particularly in my role as a parent. Becoming aware of my triggers and the core wounds that still need to be healed enables me to respond to my children in a way that validates their feelings and allows them to feel seen and heard. I grew up when children were 'seen and not heard,' so this is a huge cycle breaker for me.

- Observing my internal dialogue and my self-talk has also helped me reflect on whose voice I am actually hearing and whose language I am using. Self-talk is powerful and key to practicing self-love.

- Identifying the generational patterns and programmes which were running in the background has allowed me to interrupt them and replace them with something better, for me, for Ben, and for Ava.

- Practicing self-validation, self-regulation, and self-love has enabled me to free my children from being the source of these things for me.

- Accepting that my children are not here to fulfil my dreams, my expectations, or my ideals but to live their own unique life has enabled me to break the pattern of parental projection.

Over the past few years, I've realised that this journey back to who we were when we came here isn't easy or for the faint-hearted. It's a journey that requires a willingness to dig deep, to go within, to unlearn and relearn. It's a journey that requires us to peel back the layers of conditioning and revisit the pain and suffering. It's a journey that is messy… but for me, it's a journey that has and always will be absolutely WORTH IT!

My Mission

For the past 20 years, I have spent most of my working life with children and young people. As a Primary School Teacher and more recently as a Teen Coach Practitioner, I have come to witness the need for change. Not in the children themselves but in the parenting approaches, educational systems, and belief systems that cripple their confidence, their uniqueness, and creativity.

It is my mission to create change for children, and I envision helping parents to become conscious of who they are, and why they are the way they are, as a way of making this happen.

For anyone interested in learning more about me or how I can help I can be reached via the following links:

https://www.facebook.com/karen.cummings.568

https://www.instagram.com/karen_colquhoun_coach

About the Author

Karen Colquhoun is a qualified Primary Teacher, accredited Life Coach and Teen Coach Practitioner. She has spent the past 22 years in Primary Education with the aim of making a difference in the lives of the children in her care. Karen has experience, not only of teaching children in the way of academics, but also of teaching them about the importance of knowing who they truly are, being themselves, and loving themselves first!

As a Teen Coach, Karen loves nothing more than holding space for young people who need a safe space to just 'be' – free from judgement, expectations, and conditions. She has worked with young girls to take control of their anxiety, develop their confidence, build their self-esteem, and identify the next steps to achieving their goals.

Karen's self-development journey and discovery of spirituality helped her identify her mission in life – to create 'change for children.' In her role as a parent, she has gained an understanding of the impact that her beliefs and own childhood trauma have had, not only on her as a mum, but in all areas of her life and now seeks to support other parents of teens to become conscious, to break free from generational patterns of lack, limitation, fear, and adverse childhood experiences.

When Karen isn't teaching or coaching, her other passion in life is writing. She has written several poems, some of which have been published this year. Karen was recently awarded 'Elite Writer' status for 2022 and will have her poem featured in the upcoming 2022 Poet's Yearbook. To connect with Karen, please visit: https://facebook.com/karen.cummings.568 or

https://www.instagram.com/karen_colquhoun_coach

KATIE BOCK

The Hidden Wound that Surfaced Unexpectedly

The autumn leaves were falling, and nature was letting go while I found myself stuck on the sofa wondering, "What am I doing wrong?" It was eleven years after I walked away from the abusive relationship in which I had been stuck in for 5 years of my life, and yet my trauma was still creeping up. I could no longer shut away the unhealed parts of myself... I had to face it. The hardest part of it all was I thought I had untangled myself from the beliefs that kept me stuck in toxic relationships. My intuition was showing me that I was, in fact, still entangled, and it was time to break free.

At the beginning of 2021, I said, 'This is the year I expand the business, grow to create financial stability and double impact.' I had no idea that this statement would unfold into a whirlwind of ups and downs. In the early part of the year, I indeed was success-ful in my attempts to grow finances and impact, yet as summer neared, my grand plans started to fall apart piece by piece. By the time autumn hit, I had no income, and I felt like a failure. I spent hours each day glued to the sofa binge watching Netflix in a dis-sociated state of mind. This was the only way I could process the triggers, feelings, and sensations that were unfolding within me. My soul said, 'No more! It's time to break the chains of this story and create a new one.'

The walls began to crumble. Some might say this was a divine crumbling, and today, I would agree with them. Yet at the moment they crumbled, I did not feel that way. For years, I had invited practices into my life that I felt healed many parts of me. Yoga and meditation were the main tools I credited on my journey to heal. Yoga itself opened up my awareness and taught me how to connect within. In their own way, yoga asana and yoga philos-ophy revealed my path to healing in many areas of my life. Yoga had such a significant impact on my life that I knew I needed to share this healing gift with others.

My mission became to empower as many humans as I could. I thought I had untangled from all the wounds of the past, and I felt I could support others to do the same. Yet in those autumn moments when the crumble began, it became clear that I had more to untangle. I felt confused, lost, and deeply sad. The only option I saw in front of me was to dive in like a swan dives into the depths of the water.

As I dove into the entangled pieces of my story, I realized that every time I broke from the belief that I was unworthy, unimportant, or not good enough in one area of my life, those thoughts would show up in another part of my life. This time it showed up in the business I was building. The belief was tangled into everything I did. My people-pleaser, fixer, and perfectionist tendencies loved it! They were on fire, bright, and strong. My soul on the other hand was sad and smoldered. My inner flame was barely existent. As my awareness grew, I began to feel overwhelmed and emotionally paralyzed. I had lived with these beliefs for so long, and I thought I had broken free of them. The realization that I was still entangled in them was deflating. To untangle them seemed daunting, so I tried something I never had before. Instead of fighting my feelings and fears, I allowed myself to feel whatever came up in the moment without judgment. When the inner critic jumped in with judgment, I let it speak and chose to question the judgments and harsh words instead of just believing them. Sitting at the table with the inner critic was not easy. However, the consistent awareness and questioning I had with the inner critic was paramount to my ability to untangle. The awareness that I began to meet each moment with was ultimately what allowed me to heal these festering wounds and step into the expansion I had always wanted.

While in this state of awareness, I had surrendered in a way that I was no longer in the struggle, and I could retrace my steps backwards. I was able to observe the roots of these beliefs, love them, and rebuild some new pathways to travel when triggered in the arena of self-worth. The next light bulb moment was when I started to understand that motherhood had amplified this toxic belief I had. Everywhere you look there are the images of motherhood and womanhood as being givers, doing for others all while staying pretty, poised, and perfect. It's as if mothers and women in general are expected to be superhuman creatures with no emotions or needs of their own. At this point in my life, I had established a solid belief that I wasn't important. To embrace this ideal of motherhood did not phase me, I was already people pleasing and striving for perfection. I took it on and put everyone else before me. And I lived in that for a long time, ignoring the cues of my soul, because I was already trained to be whatever I needed to be in the moment and to make sure everyone else was okay.

You see, before I became a mother at nineteen, I walked a different path. My life was like a soap opera full of drama and chaos around me and within me. By the time I was sixteen, I already believed that I wasn't good enough, and I just wanted to be loved and to feel worthy. I wanted to matter. The combination of my belief and the desire to feel the opposite drew me to a boy who in many ways wanted the same things. But it was his traumas and stories that would tear me down to shreds. And one day, I would have to pick up those shreds to rebuild myself.

In the beginning, everything seemed fun, exciting even. We rode four wheelers, hung out with friends, and were carefree teenagers. Life was simple, but then something shifted. I cannot pinpoint when or how it happened; I can however remember the pit in my stomach, the sense to control every moment to keep myself out of harm's way, and the fear that followed me everywhere I went.

In my head, I can still hear him screaming, "No one likes you! You're a slut! What a fake bitch!" He would regularly hurl manipulative ultimatums and ridiculous demands at me. I can still feel his spit on my face and the fear that my finger would break because he bent it back so far in his anger. I know the worry of being followed, stalked, and held against my will. That time in my life was a rollercoaster taking me through terrifying loops, turns, and drops that would only serve to reinforce the belief that I wasn't worthy, I didn't matter, and I wasn't good enough.

Toxic and abusive relationships are quite often a cycle of extremes: great moments and awful moments. That's the cycle I lived in for 5 years, a continuous back and forth. I would come to adapt the subconscious need to control everything. I would learn how to pretend and hide myself. I would learn to be who I needed to be to suit the situation or people around me. I would become a shell of the dreamer I used to be.

I can remember sitting in the red Toyota as he drove after the baby basic skills class at the hospital, the one he fell asleep in and yelled at me for scheduling because it was the day after his birthday (the only day the class was held the rest of that year). I was about twenty-two weeks pregnant and very, very tired. I wanted to go home, but he wanted me to go to his house. He was already enraged and on edge, and I knew if I didn't agree to go to his house, something bad would happen. As I expected, when I expressed aloud that I wanted to go home, he started yelling.

I don't remember the words he said yet my body remembered all the moments in the past when his yelling had turned into something much worse. When I tried to breathe, I could not. I started to cry, and I could feel myself trying to breathe yet always short of a full breath in or out… I was having a panic attack. My biggest fear was the baby in my belly not receiving the oxygen he needed; I wasn't even worried about myself. It was in that moment that I realized I had to make a change. Not being able to breathe metaphorically and physically was no longer an option.

In the years that followed, I had to set clear boundaries, make tough choices, and be stronger than I ever knew possible. That often looked like saying "no" even though I was terrified to my core of someone else's reaction. It was certainly a time in my life that I stopped allowing fear to run the show and started to follow my instincts and intuition.

Everything I did, I did for the little boy I had brought into this world; every choice, every moment was for him. The lines I drew in the sand about custody and visitation were tested over and over again, yet I was able to stand strong. I was so proud of myself for being the mother who made sure her baby was safe, supported, and nurtured, yet when I reflected upon this, I felt a nagging pull of disappointment, anger, and upset.

I was deeply angry with myself for not walking away sooner. I was so proud that I walked away for that beautiful little boy and so angry that I didn't walk away years before for my own self. It was an anger that fed the wolf inside who was running with the story of 'I don't matter. I am not important. I am not worthy.' It was an anger that created a lack of self-trust. That anger became shame which made it even harder to love myself.

All these experiences built upon the story I was living in, the wound that was festering within. Despite living a seemingly joyful life, I was very unhappy and unfulfilled. I was looking for someone or something outside of myself to make me feel worthy, important, and enough, and it was not working.

When the walls began to crumble in my business, I discovered I was looking outside of myself to shift that story because it wasn't a story that I was willing to live in (yet I *was* living it and believing it and making choices based around it). But there was never anything outside of myself that could make me feel important, worthy, or valuable because I wasn't treating myself as such in my everyday life. I was unconsciously manifesting these experiences that just kept affirming the story. Not to mention, I was going on autopilot, and I ignored the cues from my body that tried to show me this was no longer working. It was a foundation of awareness, understanding, and embodiment that allowed me to empower myself to make choices that negated the story I was living and rewrite a new story in order to heal and expand.

Once in a coaching session, I shared, "I feel as if I've unleashed this can of worms, and I just want to put the lid back on and pretend it never existed." In that moment I was so over the process of healing, so over the struggle of realizing what I was actually feeling. It created a heaviness that I was just ready to let go of, but, for some reason, I couldn't. When I look back to this moment, I know I just needed more time. I had to sit with triggers a bit longer. I had to bring more awareness to the wounds. I had to feel the sensations in my body and move energy through my body.

The moment I released that heaviness was a moment I completely chose myself. I embodied the new belief that I matter, I am important, and I am worthy. It was also the affirmation that I trusted myself and the choices I make. This happened when my intuition told me to quit my job, a job that paid the bills, yet I was very unhappy in. It took me two weeks to do it, but I did it. The moment I quit I fully embodied a new belief that I was important, enough, and worthy while also affirming trust in myself. I had a full body reaction. My entire body shook for 10-15 minutes. It was the release of my festering wound. It was the untangling of old, worn-out beliefs. I would never be the same. The chains were broken, my mind was free. I believed in myself again, and I knew without a doubt that I was worthy, important, and enough. The feeling was magical (cliché, I know, but there's no other way for me to describe it).

A caterpillar spends its whole life nourishing itself getting enough energy and enough food to turn into a butterfly. And once it reaches that point, it wraps itself in a cocoon of darkness and turns into a complete goo before its wings grow, and it morphs into that brilliant, beautiful butterfly. Sometimes you just have to get into the cocoon, into the goo, and sit in the darkness because that is how you grow your wings and become the brilliant, beautiful butterfly that you are.

Practices To Support You on Your Journey

The mind loves stories, it loves drama. It's the stories you choose to believe that govern the flow of your mind, your ego, your intuition, your entire life. Your thoughts create feelings which create actions which create your life experiences, circumstances, all of it. What is often forgotten is that you hold the power within to rewrite the story in any moment you choose.

I say it's time to remember you have a choice! These are the practices that supported me as I walked through the process of untangling myself and breaking free. They are also the practices I use daily to support my own well-being, mental clarity, and inner freedom.

Practice Mindfulness and Embodiment

For so long, I sat in autopilot completely unaware of how the wounds within were bleeding out into my life. The moment I turned the light back on was the moment I gave myself the power to heal the wounds and shift the belief/story. When you become aware, you take back the power.

Mindfulness is the state of being aware or conscious. Embodiment is the state of being in your body.

Both are essential to well-being, healing, freedom, and transformation. When you become aware and embodied you discover the cues of your body, your intuition, and your soul. This is also how you release old beliefs, feelings, and wounds. Everything lives in your body, so as you tap into your body mindfully, you can create the space to process and release what is stuck.

Through the practices of mindfulness and embodiment, you create a foundation made of bricks that inspire stability, safety, and understanding. The foundation is built on knowledge you learn about yourself as you turn the light on and connect inward. When you get to know yourself, you begin to understand why you do the things you do, and that is powerful. Not only is it powerful, it can also provide a sense of comfort which is what you need to release and rewrite any belief or story of the mind. To know what triggers you, to know what feels good for you and lifts you up, to know your boundaries is soothing to the ego and nervous system. The more you know about yourself, the simpler it becomes to understand your needs and the path to inner freedom, peace, and joy.

The best thing I ever did for myself was to start a 2-minute pause practice. I encourage you to try it for yourself. Every two hours or so pause for 2 minutes, bring your awareness to your breath, the sensations in your body, or stretch where your body is asking you to. This small pause wires your brain to be awake and aware and in your body. Over time, you create a subconscious habit that will serve you greatly by providing wisdom and guidance because the pauses create space for you to tune in and receive.

Practice Acceptance

The most important part of mindfulness and embodiment is to practice non-judgment. There is no right or wrong, good, or bad... there simply just *is*. Two truths can co-exist just as light, and darkness can co-exist. For many years, I had much joy in my life while I was also unfulfilled, sad, and lost. I do not claim a perfect life today, nor do I want one. What I know with absolute certainty is the ability to be with myself without judgment is how I recognize when old beliefs, stories, and triggers show up which allows me to choose how to respond instead of being stuck in the struggle of it.

All of the beliefs, stories, and triggers that live within were created at one time to serve you. They just no longer work for you at this moment in time. For years, my belief that I was not worthy kept me safe. It taught me to be a people pleaser, so I could survive.

When survival was not threatened, I didn't need it anymore. As I no longer needed to be protected, the belief became a block. Without acceptance, I would not have been able to release the block, and I would still be in the struggle. The punishment and judgment you place upon yourself will only keep you stuck. Acceptance and empathy melt the ice for you to flow with what you feel and who you are evolving to be.

One of my favorite methods for acceptance is the ancient Hawaiian healing practice Ho'oponopono. The process of ho'oponopono is to cut the connection (attachment) in order to rejuvenate relationships with the self and others. It translates "to move back into balance." The script is below. You start by saying "I'm sorry" to acknowledge the actions, thoughts, and emotions that are or have caused conflict within you. Then you say "Please forgive me" to request an amends with your higher self, the universe, and the divine. Followed by "Thank you" to show gratitude as the thoughts, actions, and emotions are cleared. You end with "I love you" to show love to yourself and all life in the universe. Repeat it as many times as you feel called to.

I'm Sorry.
Please Forgive Me.
Thank You.
I Love You.

Make Conscious Choices

What I have learned over time is that power is choice. You always have the power to make a choice and another choice. There is no limit to the number of choices you can make. Choice is infinite! The small conscious choices support you when it becomes time for big choices. Little moments create massive shifts.

I shared earlier in the chapter that I was a people pleaser, perfectionist, and over-giver which often led me to over-work and take on too much. As I became mindful and embodied, I began to notice the cues that told me I needed to stop and rest. When I ignored these cues, the result was usually several days of exhaustion and feeling powerless. Yet when I listened and chose to rest for a short time, I felt powerful, and I learned where I needed boundaries. I began to empower myself through small conscious choices, and piece by piece, I became untangled.

What small conscious choices can you make that support you on your journey? I ask you to make them and empower yourself!

The moral of the story is entanglement can happen behind the scenes, and even when you think you have untangled, there might be more to explore. Remember to create space to connect to yourself through mindfulness and embodiment. And don't forget your power to choose acceptance!

About the Author

Katie Bock is the creator of the Illuminations card deck and the host of Living Free and Fulfilled, a podcast with real talk about life, spirituality and living life your way. She is passionate about creating space and support for those who wish to rediscover their power, inner wisdom, and magic.

At age 19, Katie became a mom, and she is now the proud mama of three boys. She survived an abusive relationship, grew from her wounds, and continues that healing journey every day because she believes there is always space to expand.

In 2013, she graduated with a degree in Massage Therapy which led into yoga. Since then, she has become a 200 HR Registered Yoga Teacher, Holistic Health Coach, and Holy Fire/Karuna/Crystal Reiki Master. Katie combines her knowledge in yoga, meditation, energy work, trauma-informed care, and mindset to create containers for empowerment, transformation, and growth. To connect with Katie, please visit:

https://www.katiebock.com

FB, Instagram, TikTok: @katiebockyoga

Podcast: Living Free and Fulfilled on all listening platforms and https://www.katiebock.com/podcast

KATIE CAREY

Releasing Toxic Money and Love Wounds

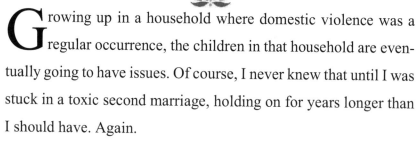

G rowing up in a household where domestic violence was a regular occurrence, the children in that household are eventually going to have issues. Of course, I never knew that until I was stuck in a toxic second marriage, holding on for years longer than I should have. Again.

A child who feels unsafe and hurt, is not allowed to have an opinion, or ask for what they need, will do whatever they can to protect themselves. Most of my childhood was spent shut away in my bedroom, and trust me, I was safer for that. But because I was never allowed to stay at friend's houses, I didn't know that my experiences in my home were wrong, and as a child in the 1970's living in a rough neighbourhood, violence was the usual solution to people's problems. Schools used violence and encouraged parents to discipline their children with violence, (especially in the Irish Catholic School that we attended) and that's exactly what they did.

I know that my parents were just following the norm for their cultures and societal expectations of the day with a bit of added over-protection thrown in because they already suffered the loss of two stillborn babies – one right before me, and one right after me. I was a "rainbow baby."

By the time I was a 14-year-old teenager, the hormones had kicked in, and I had my first teenage crush. I remember being called "frigid" by some of the boys and many other cruel names. I did not look my age; in fact, I looked years younger which is why I was chosen to play a 12-year-old on a TV series when I was 15. I did not even have my first period until I was 16. I chose not to have sex with boys or do the other things that my teen friends were doing. I did not smoke and wouldn't go near drugs, but I did drink alcohol (which my dad gave to me as a 14-year-old) to give me courage when singing on stage. My Dad could sing and would not dare get on a stage to do that himself, so he felt I needed that for what he called Dutch courage.

I had no freedom outside of school apart from after school activities like drama, music, and gymnastics. I loved school. Not all aspects of school, but my school was great at encouraging us to

146

do the things we loved. I have never witnessed another school like that, and my children went to several schools as we were a military family.

A romantic relationship for me as a teenager was simply not a possibility; my dad would have killed me. In fact, he told me that I must not marry until I am at least 30 years old, and any boys who came near, he would be dealing with! I had already decided that I was going to be an actress and a singer. Unlike many of the girls I knew, I had no plans to marry or have children.

I was beyond infatuated. I held on to this crush for three years between the ages of 14 and 17. While most teenage girls have crushes, I see now that my feelings for this boy were displaying much deeper roots from within my soul. I was desperate to be seen. I felt unworthy, unlovable, not good enough, always having to push myself to be the best because there would also be trouble at home if I weren't! I seriously wanted and planned to end my life on two occasions in my teens. (I have not really shared this publicly until now.)

In May 1986, I auditioned for a place in the National Student Theatre company. I was invited following my performance at the National Student Drama Festival. The audition was in London, and I was in this crowded room, and he was all I could see! He stood out, as he walked into the room even though there were hundreds of people around us. Then, we were all sent downstairs to the audition room, a few at a time and quite bizarrely, we were immediately paired up together to sing a duet.

"Rose Rose, Rose, Rose, shall I ever see the red? I'll Marry that thou will and thou but still." I can still hear his sultry voice clearly in my mind all these years later! Our voices blended divinely. I was immediately hooked.

After the audition for the Edinburgh festival, we chatted and ended up sharing the train most of the way home. He told me about his dream to be a writer and pulled out some of his short stories. He had huge dreams, almost as crazy as mine, and I loved that.

We went our separate ways that day, and then I heard a few weeks later that I had won a place at the National Student Theatre Company. The play was called "Sammy's Magic Garden," which meant that I would be away in London and Edinburgh all summer.

In July, towards the end of our London showing in Battersea, the beautiful man from the audition in May, appeared at a rehearsal in London. I felt that rush of energy again. It was powerful. What was it about him? He was like no one else I had ever met. I loved being in his company. Later, we would do the Edinburgh Festival. I was only seventeen, so I shouldn't have been drinking alcohol, but it was already something I had been doing at weekends with my parents' encouragement and permission back home.

I was the only member of the National Student Theatre Company who was not in drama school or a university student. It was quite a miracle that I had been offered a part, and this gorgeous young man was always there to save the day. He walked me home to my digs, made sure I was safe and not taken advantage of by anyone. I was head over heels in love. We were inseparable that summer. I was his biggest fan, faithfully watching his show from the audience. To be honest, I was stalking him looking back at that, but he seemed to enjoy the attention!

That summer ended, and he very kindly explained to me the reality that we could only ever be friends. Neither of us could drive. We lived hundreds of miles from each other, and it was impossible. We said our goodbyes on the 31st of August 1986. This date became synchronistic in future relationships.

One year to that date, I would meet the man who would become my first husband and the father of my children. He was in the same battalion as my dad. I thought my dad would love this and approve, but he did not. He warned me not to marry him, but I was young and naïve, and of course my dad did not tell me why I shouldn't marry a soldier. The fact that he had been one and knew exactly what I was letting myself in for was another matter. I thought I was in love. Of course, I did not have a clue then what love was. My experience of it so far had been pretty shit. I was desperate to get away from home at that age, and I had already given up on my dreams. The Edinburgh Festival heartbreak probably had something to do with that. I had to get back to the real world, where money was so hard to come by for a poverty-stricken council estate city girl like me. I had no chance without money. My parents would remind me of this often and encouraged me to leave my acting behind and "get a real job and save up for the Drama school, as suggested by my Agent."

Meeting my first husband took me on a whirlwind of excitement that someone wanted me. Many people had left me feeling unwanted by this stage, so maybe this was it. We had lots of fun before we married when I was only twenty years old. He would come home when he could, and we would go out. Our relationship was all about going out, drinking, partying, and having fun dancing. I do not regret any of it, not a moment, because between us we created the most incredible human beings – our three children.

I stopped saving for drama school because I knew it was impossible to continue acting while being married to a soldier. For a few years, we lived a life that was all about working hard for money and partying hard whenever we could, until I was made redundant, and we were posted to Northern Ireland. After trying to have a baby for a year, I became pregnant with my first child.

I loved being a mum, but I was alone often, eventually with three children ages 0-4 in a military flat in Germany, where drama was the norm, and I became very serious. We moved thirteen times in eleven years. I never felt settled anywhere, until we bought my current home, where I've been living for almost twenty years.

Depression is something that I experienced several times throughout my life, but I never really knew that until I realised in 2005 that I needed a drink during the week a little too often. I suddenly remembered how alcohol had killed my father at the young age of 48 and took myself off to the doctors, where I was prescribed antidepressants for the first time. My husband ridiculed me in front of my children for needing medication. I had been unhappy in that marriage for several years. I felt disconnected emotionally, unloved, and unsupported. Life felt like an uphill struggle.

There was never enough money, and I was always trying to find ways to earn and contribute, because I felt so shit having to ask for money and not having my own. Eventually, I found a business opportunity that fit around my children and that I loved: selling on eBay.

At the time, I was working from home from 6 am until 11:30 pm. Even though I was able to work around my children, I struggled being the only adult with them the majority of the time. My husband was often away, and the load became too heavy for me to carry alone. I became even more depressed, and that marriage soon ended when I really discovered what my intuition had been trying to tell me, that I had ignored for so long.

I divorced him very quickly and shockingly (now I look back at this), within a few months of telling my husband that I wanted a divorce, I moved in with the man who would become husband number two. At first, everything seemed wonderful. The children all liked him, and this man could not do enough for us. I felt that he loved us all. Then, one thing after another would happen to change that.

I had to go out and get a real job to take on the mortgage, as my self-employment, although great in the spring and summer was not great in autumn and winter. I started a new job in my village, worked there for six months, and came home crying every day. I hated it so much. My boss was a bully.

We had not long been married, and we had huge plans for what we were going to do with our home. Not long after, I would discover the drinks hamper I had won at Christmas was almost gone! I flew into a rage, launching a bowl across the kitchen. (I still haven't changed those broken tiles yet, which serve as a constant reminder to me of that outburst. It is on my upleveling my home list of things to be done very soon though).

The thoughts persisted in my mind. I was distraught.

"My husband is an alcoholic! What have I done?" I had indeed attracted the very thing that I most dreaded right into my life. I lost my father to alcoholism, which was aa blessing really, that my children did not have to get to know him. He was still my dad and losing him hurt a lot. I had spent most my earlier life wanting to save him.

As a small girl, I remember nursing him over the toilet when he vomited, rubbing his back, and crying because I just wanted him to get back to being the happy and healthy dad I used to know. I was determined that this would not happen with any of my husbands. And here I was, right back in the same situation again playing a different role. For years, he would go around in cycles of being sober and then not. I felt like I was in a dark hole that I could not climb out of. In fact, I have watched the Maid on Netflix recently, a story about a woman with a partner who was also an addict. I could easily recognise that dark hole that she kept finding herself in of both wanting to help the man she loved while not wanting to hurt herself anymore.

In 2010, I started an admin job at the local hospital, and in the first week there, I was invited to meditation every Thursday during lunchtime. I was not happy at that job or at home, but I lived for that meditation session, which was the beginning of my journey of attempting to climb out of that dark hole.

One day as I was leaving the office for my session, my boss remarked, "You're weird!" My husband told me, "I think you are losing your mind! You have become obsessed with Abraham Hicks!" (I found Abraham after reading several of David Knight's spiritual books. Thankyou David! David has written a chapter in Evolving on Purpose: Co-creating with the Divine, being released in autumn 2022).

By 2011, I found myself studying holistic therapies and became attuned to Reiki. I loved it, and something shifted. I would spend the next few years staying in that job because I needed the money, whilst also studying therapies and an Open University bachelor's degree to try to improve my prospects of earning more.

In 2013, I set up a local mental health charity called STAGES. Much of the studying I did was to help my husband and people like us who struggled without support. While studying psychology, counselling, and psychotherapy, I started going down the rabbit hole regarding mental health studies. I realised something profound about my own thinking. I had mental health conditions too and most certainly was suffering with undiagnosed PTSD.

Thankfully, mindfulness appeared in my world through the charity, and a drama occurred where I was left without a Mindfulness teacher. People who came to support the charity kept leaving in dramatic ways. There was a theme of me being left to do it all on my own, and me feeling disappointed. When they left, I felt that I would have to step up and teach the Mindfulness courses myself, because I could not rely on anyone else. I studied diplomas in Mindfulness, Mindful Mental Health, CBT and Mindful Nutrition, parallel to my degree, running the charity and working full-time and trying to support my teenagers and a mentally unwell husband.

I became compassionate and unconditionally loving about my husband's issues. Although deep down, I felt an inner resentment that everything was down to me. I had so many years of being the responsible one since early childhood. After bringing up three children, feeling worn down by two husbands, and carrying the burden of everyone else's dramas and problems at the charity, my body had begun to show me that she had had enough of all the chasing and carrying the weight of the world. I got to the point of being ill-health retired at age 48 with multiple joint osteoarthritis and fibromyalgia. My body forced me to really slow down!

In August 2017, (exactly five years ago as I am writing this chapter) during one of his relapses that usually lasted for months at a time or even years, an incident occurred that was so huge that I could not ignore the toxicity in my relationship any longer, and I told my ex-husband to leave. It was not easy to leave him homeless because I thought that I really loved him! I had also learned enough to know that I had to create boundaries now!

It took me another three years to completely untangle myself from that relationship, particularly as my charity was also supporting him. After all, he was the reason that I created that charity! Lisa Phillips, an author in this book, helped me to navigate my own inner child's feelings, and during a session with her, it became apparent that everything I had been feeling about him were feelings I had about my dad! I felt unloved, unsupported, frustrated, unsafe, disappointed. In fact, there was a much longer list!

I was running the charity and struggling to keep afloat. There was never enough money or support to do all that I wanted to do to make a real impact, and it became a source of major struggle, drama, and conflict. My financial struggles became a massive weight on my shoulders. Ironically, during the first year of the charity, I needed surgery for a rotator cuff tear, so I needed to take pain killers for six months just to enable me to keep going to work (to a job I hated) while waiting for that surgery!

And of course, there were other people's opinions about my relationship and my health coming at me from their versions and opinions of my reality, which I cared way too much about, especially when trying to be taken seriously about running an "alternative" mental health charity! My life became a massive source of resentment, and I was deeply entangled with the weight of other people's serious life problems and needing to be there for everyone, on top of my own dysfunctional relationship issues, even though I was there to teach mindfulness and share reiki and give holistic therapies! I was, without a doubt, a seriously wounded healer! During my studies in mental health that were to help my husband, I discovered that I had an ACE score (Adverse Childhood Experiences) of 8 out of 10, worse than most of the people I was trying to help! In October 2019, I made two major life changing decisions while on Lisa's course: I asked for a divorce, and I closed the charity!

I had come across a post online by Denise Duffield-Thomas about her money bootcamp, and through this, I recognised my money patterns that I had carried my whole life. Mindfulness is a great tool. I noticed my money patterns and how my emotions were linked to what was going on in my personal finances and the charity finances. When I was feeling great, the money would roll in, and when I was not, doors would close, and I would have to find a way to keep going myself. It has been a four-year journey to really get to grips with this. I trained in EFT to get to the root of the visceral reactions in my body around money. Trust me, they are enormously powerful when you've struggled with a lack of it since childhood.

In April 2020, I came across Joanna Hunter, my current spiritual business coach, and learned a lot of valuable information from her and still do, recently joining her Frequency of Money Summer School. I have been determined to master this one and keep on reminding myself, because it is so easy to get caught up in the lack mindset of the world around us!

It was author Katische's age and past life regressions that really shifted something huge for me! You can hear the full session on her podcast. I had three months in my business where zero income was coming in, and I now had regular business bills to pay as well as my living costs. I had to seek debt management advice. Then, I saw Katische offering her past life regression service. I knew that was where I needed to go next, and instantly as if by magic, Katische came into my inbox offering me the sessions in return for her using them on her podcast! This was an easy decision for me! The universe was trying to show me that I needed to go deeper. I had avoided past life regression for a decade. Clearly because I was worried about what other people might think about that!

The audition experience for the "Edinburgh Festival" did come through an age regression session with *Entangled No More* contributing author, Katische, on her podcast a few months ago, called "The Infinite Life," if you want to go and listen to that full session. You will get to hear me sing the song.

I have also discussed what happened in later life in a podcast episode on my Soulful Valley podcast with my guest Allen Klein. The young man from the Edinburgh Festival ended up moving into my village which is nowhere near where either of us lived back then, just after my first marriage ended and staying in touch by sending Christmas cards to each other for almost twenty years until both of our first marriages ended. We both married our second partners in the same year. Sadly, I heard that he passed away just before the pandemic.

In the sessions with Katische, money stories that I was not consciously aware of came through me that I didn't realise had such an impact on me. I had trained in various modalities where I had to write out lists of financial traumatic experiences that I remembered consciously. These events, such as my last gig as a singer, believing my husband's anxious belief that they would not pay me, had led to me retiring from singing. I also uncovered past life experiences where I had a brother murdered over money, a lifetime where I had been killed for stealing food for my five children, lives where I had been wealthy, and a lifetime where I was with a man that still loved me and was there for me and my children when I lay on my deathbed saying goodbye to them. I fully resonate with the spiritual aspect of this, but if you cannot manage to get your head around this concept logically, consider the ancestral DNA of these types of fears carried down to us through our ancestors biologically. They have become our instincts!

Days after my last session with Katische, I had major pain in the middle of the night. I was laid out on my bathroom floor in agony for three hours. I could not get to my phone, and no one could hear my screams. When it finally eased long enough for me to crawl into the bedroom, I looked at my phone and an author from my first book had messaged asking to join us in the next *Evolving on Purpose* book. It was hilarious when I told Katische that I had released kidney stones in one day, along with a three-month money receiving block! This was also a full spiral, as my disabilities began with three years of kidney stones that I could not release or have removed! Katische shared an article about the spiritual connection of kidney stones to money. Then on the date she released our first episode live on 11th April, I had my first date with my now boyfriend who I manifested out of nowhere with a simple line I said out loud to my son.

"Maybe that's where I've gone wrong, maybe I need an Alan in my life!"

Magically we connected the next morning after we had both been following intuitive nudges. He had just moved back to Corby, my local town from 200 miles away, having left the area 20 years ago when I moved here. The synchronicities we had going on between us were off the charts obvious to me! I also went on to have my best week in my business, better than my best month previously this month! I am so excited about the future where I get to choose to create my life while *Evolving on Purpose and* choosing to be *Entangled No More.* I am enjoying sharing my journey of *Becoming the Manifesting Diva: Creating Ripples While I Flow,* whilst changing my *Money* stories of the past by *Unplugging from the Lack Matrix!*

About the Author

Katie Carey, an International best-selling author, is the CEO of Katie Carey Media LTD, the founder of the Soulful Valley Publishing House, and the host of the Soulful Valley podcast, a Top 0.5% globally ranked podcast.

Katie uses both the podcast and the multi-author books as a platform to help metaphysical coaches, energy healers, authors and conscious creators to elevate their work, so that the people they are here to serve can find them.

Formerly the founder of STAGES, an alternative mental health charity for seven years, Katie is an advocate for Mental Health and Emotional Wellbeing, particularly since her own health was affected when she was ill-health retired because of disabilities at the age of 48 due to conditions brought about by trauma.

Katie loves blending science and spirituality together and collaborates with people on the same wavelength in her multi-author books. Most authors have stories of synchronicities that led to them writing in books with Katie. Katie's aim is to bring these concepts and ideas to more people who are seeking ways to support their own mental, spiritual, emotional, and physical wellbeing.

Katie has a history of working in TV, Radio, and Theatre as an actress and singer, which she manifested into her life in her teens. Katie lives in a Northamptonshire Village in the UK and is a Mum to three adult children and "Nanny Katie" to her grandchildren. Katie intends to make it her life's work to educate people to find healthier solutions and break free from ancestral, toxic, and generational patterns of lack and trauma. Katie is passionate about raising consciousness and currently does this with her work as a Mentor, Coach, Podcaster, Author, Publisher, and through her songs and poetry.

If you would like to collaborate with Katie in one of her multi-author books or to write your own solo book, you can contact Katie below:

- Website: https://www.soulfulvalley.com
- Email: soulfulvalleypodcast@gmail.com
- FB, Twitter, IG, and LinkedIn @soulfulvalley
- Podcast: https://apple.co/3BkJdkn

KATISCHE HABERFIELD

Disentangling Limiting Belief
from Other Lifetimes

Have you ever noticed the amount of time you spend in your head or all the entangled thoughts that weave in and out of your mind that you take as gospel? Some are helpful, yet some are downright rude. Most of our thoughts contain threads to the beliefs we hold about ourselves.

These beliefs are stored in our sub- and superconscious mind and are based on our experiences in our current life and our other lives. They become what we hold true about ourselves and begin to limit our life because our conscious mind uses our sub- and superconscious mind to reference everything that we do in life to see if it fits and holds true with what we know about ourselves.

One of the brilliant and beautiful things about the human mind is that it comes with a built-in protection system. It's invisible and, at times, feels impenetrable. It's the Ego who controls the conscious mind and is like a bouncer at a nightclub for the subconscious mind and the superconscious mind.

But the secrets are held at the subconscious and the superconscious level. The subconscious mind is the holding room for all the experiences and the emotions that you have in your lifetime.

The superconscious mind is the eternal mind stream. It is the mind stream that directly links you to your Higher Self and to source. It contains all thoughts and emotions from every single "lifetime" here and everywhere else.

So, if we look at what we believe, then we need to look at several levels of beliefs.

If your subconscious mind disagrees with your conscious mind, it will overrule your conscious mind. And if your subconscious mind disagrees or even concurs with your superconscious mind, then the superconscious mind is the winner. Whatever the superconscious mind believes, that is your human reality. And it is a reality that is replayed over and over again, lifetime after lifetime after lifetime.

Let me tell you a story about a client of mine, with her permission, that illustrates how entangled our thoughts and beliefs of this life are with our previous lives, and the consequences that can play out.

Vivian felt like a fraud. She was encouraging others to tap into their spiritual wisdom, but she could not tap into her own. She was afraid of the consequences of tapping into her spiritual wisdom and relied on the spiritual wisdom of her teachers. And that spiritual wisdom lasted for only so long. It was wonderful, but when that teacher released her and told her to go forward and take the teachings further, she froze deeper and deeper and went into a great state of depression because she knew she was afraid of tapping into this spiritual knowledge again.

And this fear she felt, was then felt by those who were attracted to her work, and they began to have doubts of their own and wondered if it was safe for them to dig into not only their own knowledge but into Vivian's wisdom.

People fear change most of all, and they allow themselves to stagnate rather than step forward boldly into the unknown, especially if the unknown has an element of danger.

The clients dried up. They stayed around Vivian and interacted with her, but they delayed purchasing, until Vivian could no longer pay the rent. Vivian went from earning over $100,000 per year to nothing when we started working together. Over the process of 8 sessions, we worked through many lives, but will just cover a couple here.

We went back in time, to a life in Egypt where Vivian was a male scribe. As a scribe, he had undertaken a lifelong vow to protect the spiritual wisdom and secrets of his people with his life. This vow was a binding spell of sorts. It came with great privilege and responsibility, but also great sacrifice, and it could not be undone.

There was a great personal danger that came with being the scribe who wrote down the sacred knowledge of the Pharaoh and the danger associated with the protection of these scrolls. The scrolls contained secret knowledge about RA, the Sun god. Only a few people could handle this sacred knowledge. There was great danger to the Kingdom if anyone else read them and found out the secrets. There was also great danger to his family and himself if he was ever caught by the enemy.

Danger always comes with an element of fear, and his greatest fear was being captured by the enemy and being forced to give away the secrets. And because the mind focuses on what it thinks about and especially what it fears, in time it transpired that this did eventually happen. He was captured by the enemy and tortured.

But no matter how great the physical pain or the mental pain, he did not reveal the great spiritual secrets. And so, they decided to break him, by making him watch the death of his family and his children. They were captured and tortured in front of him, and even though he would have done anything to save them, he could not save them because of the vow to protect the secrets. And so they died, and the enemy still tortured him. But still he did not reveal the secrets, and so they killed him. He paid the ultimate price by sacrificing his life to protect the spiritual knowledge.

Vivian learned in this life that it was dangerous to be a carrier of sacred spiritual wisdom and this became a limiting belief. Her mindstream still carried the memories of watching her children be tortured and murdered, and it told her in her current lifetime that it was dangerous to follow her soul's calling. If she did, something terrible would happen to her children and her family.

But of course, we no longer live in Ancient Egypt, and these are different times. There is no threat to Vivian, and spiritual secrets are revealed every day. Her mind begged to differ, because if she could not earn money then surely something bad would happen to her family. And to add to her stresses, there was the modern equivalent of a "witch hunt" happening in her mind and her physical reality.

The Tax Collectors were "after her." In the here and now, in the current lifetime, Vivian was behind in her taxes. It's easy to do this when self-employed. The money we put aside from each client's payment to cover taxes often gets spent on the groceries and necessities of life, thinking we will have time and the ability to pay it later when the annual tax return is due.

The collectors had given her a deadline and were even contacting her clients to take the money out of any incoming payments before she received it! She was ashamed and embarrassed and felt like a complete fraud because she was teaching about infinite possibilities and abundance, and her abundance was shrinking all around her, and actually she was living the opposite life. She was drowning in bills and shame and self-hatred. Who was she to teach this when she could not embody it? She had embodied it very successfully, but that was a year ago, and then the tax notice was delivered, and in an instant her world changed.

You see, when she received the information about the tax collection, her mind stream took her directly back to a lifetime when she was the subject of a real witch hunt. And even though she was not consciously aware of this, her mind was checking back, referencing this similar parallel situation, and making the situation worse. The mind only knows emotion and thoughts, and the emotion of fear was now very great.

I regressed Vivian back to a lifetime as Jane, an old lady who was a healer, a real witch, who used botanicals to heal the sick and infirm. In that lifetime, she was a great healer, but the healing was done in secret because society was afraid of women with healing abilities. And so, she sat in the shadows whilst trying to shine her inner light. But the fear crept in, and one day, she was walking near the markets, collecting items for her potions, and her mind was in a negative state, hoping that this next batch of potions would work for her clients. She was ruminating about her worst nightmare, that her potions might be mixed the wrong way or that a bad batch of herbs might lead to her clients being harmed, and then someone would find her and kill her.

Nearby, a little girl had died. Her name was Angel, and she was only 15. She had an undiagnosed heart problem which was manifesting in the bloating of her body. She was on an errand to the market when her heart suddenly stopped. It was a great shock to her system to find that suddenly she had died. She didn't know why or what happened. She felt lost, scared, and afraid, and she missed her moment to see the light and the rainbow bridge and cross over to heaven.

The little girl wandered aimlessly around the marketplace and tried to ask for help, but, of course, her body was no longer with her, she was spirit in form, and no one heard her cries for help, and then she saw Jane. She could see that she would help, and so she asked ever so sweetly if they could be together. And Jane could not see a reason why not, and so she agreed. Angel attached herself to Jane, their fears joined, and they became one.

The immediate impact was that suddenly her fears about the potions became stronger, and one day, the fears came true. The potions began to harm the patients and not heal them. Jane was arrested, taken to trial, and killed for being a witch. Jane died in distress, overwhelmed with wondering what had gone wrong? She had intended no harm. She had pure intentions, but she had ended up hurting her clients and her worst fears had come true. She had let down her entire lineage and become an embarrassment to herself and her community.

Taking Vivian back into these two lifetimes she discovered that actually, the potions had not hurt the clients, what had affected the clients was that their mindstream had connected to the fears radiating out from Jane and from Angel, and they had absorbed those fears and their mindstreams had become infected so to speak and these fears caused the potions to react negatively to their bodies because they suddenly had become afraid of the potions.

Their minds were their own worst enemy. They had let fear take control.

And so, when it came to incarnate in this lifetime as Vivian, those fears were forgotten, until Vivian decided to step into the light and to tap into her spiritual knowledge. For a while she was able to block these superconscious thought streams and achieve her goals, but the minute she was triggered at the superconscious level, she allowed the fears stemming from these lives to resurface.

Guilt that did not belong to her, rose to the surface. Fears that were not hers, raised their ugly heads again, and she began to lose sleep at night. Clients were no longer attracted to her, and, worst of all, she began to feel like a fraud.

When we allowed both of the soul counterparts of Vivian, the people who she had been in other lifetimes to cross over again and tap into the wisdom of their inner wise adult or higher self, they were no longer afraid. They could see the limiting beliefs and the vows that they created based on their experiences and were able to release them into the white light of spirit.

Vivian has reprogrammed her mind to accept the following statements as truth and her reality.

I am safe.

Everybody is safe in the end.

I am loyal.

I am courageous.

I have the strength to follow what I believe in.

She also gained the knowledge that it is now time for the secret spiritual wisdom to be brought back into the world again.

Vivian is not alone in experiencing lifetimes with limiting beliefs. I know this from my own personal experience. I believe that if you are going to teach something, you have to walk the talk, and so I am very public with sharing my own personal past life realisations on my podcast.

Here's an example of a spiritual lifetime of mine that I uncovered over two sessions with different practitioners, one a Quantum Healer and the other an Akashic Records Practitioner. Each session revealed a different part of the story of the one lifetime.

The intention behind the sessions were to uncover the reason for my issues with authority figures and to find out how I was self-punishing and sabotaging. I have never been in trouble with the law, but I struggle mentally with accepting authority of people who know less than me but are in higher positions of power than me. I also was struggling with visibility on social media and not having the courage to tell my story and be vulnerable.

This story takes us back in time to England, to London around 1423 AD. When I was a baby, I was abandoned by my mother and father at birth. I was placed on the steps of what we now call Westminster Abbey and left out in the cold. It was a much smaller Abbey then and the remnants still exist in the undercroft areas of today's Abbey. You don't have to feel too sorry for me; it was quite common back then, and the Monks would take in the babies and the world saw how the babies were looked after and how they lived in the house of God, and became in due time, Monks themselves.

However, life behind doors is always a different story and many of those incarnated on earth now with an aversion to organised religion will be able to tell you a story of what life was really like.

It was cold, damp, and dark, and from the moment we rose til the second our head hit the straw at night, our every waking hour was filled with prayer, study, and punishment for our sins.

My sin was abandonment, the act of being abandoned. I was therefore unloveable, and constantly reminded of this from the other Monks, despite the fact that I knew God loved me.

I was alone even though I was in the House of God.

But the people he had assigned to look after me did not, and they made me go outside each morning with a bowl and beg for food. I was not worthy of the food in the Abbey. And the rich would give me scraps and keep walking, never making eye contact. For they were more interested in the intellectual discussions of theology that they were privy to, as they were financial benefactors of the Abbey. They sponsored the publication of the beautiful hand-created manuscripts, and, for this, they were assured eternal salvation, a prize position in the pews and access to the best talents of the scholars.

I was always hungry, always cold, always lonely, and always afraid. I saw the irony of it all. I saw the abundance in the Abbey and the lack where I was involved, and I wondered, "Why me?"

When I was older, they introduced me to the concept of self-punishment in the corporal sense. "We come from sin," they said, "and live sinful lives and the way to eternal life is by asking for forgiveness by showing exactly how sorry you were." And they didn't mean to get down on your knees and pray or go "confession".

They gave me whips with burrs on them, and I was told to raise it high and strike my back over and over again until it bled, and I felt absolved of my sins.

Except I couldn't do it.

I knew this is not what our Father in Heaven wanted, and I couldn't tell you why I knew it, but I did with every inch of my soul.

And so, they whipped me, for me. It would become a daily routine. Morning meeting in the circular room and then flagellation to absolve sins. To this day, I cannot be in a round room without getting dizzy and wanting to faint.

At some point in time, it became normal, and I gave into it. I lost my resistance and the voice of Jesus faded from my mind.

Before I had heard him speak over and over into my ears, "Forgive them, Father, for they know not what they do." But now, with time, I became subdued, and this punishment became normalised.

I learned not to contradict the Monks when their spiritual gibberish contradicted the teachings that were contained in my mindstream. I learned not to seek out the forbidden books in the library, the unspoken ones that contradicted their sermons and spoke of the hidden knowledge I had inside my mind and heart.

And for the next 700 years, in each lifetime, I repeated that which was ingrained in my mind. I have sinned, I am not worthy, I contain no new knowledge, I am not special, and I need to punish myself before others punish me.

I had issues with authority and felt immense disdain. I did not clash out loud, only in my mind and in private. I felt I did not fit in, and I knew I did not want to attract attention, so I preferred to be unremarkable, even though the universe fought for the opposite to be so.

Spiritual, financial, and emotional poverty (not abundance) was the energy that I connected to. When finally, my conscious mind screamed enough, you are smart, you understand how the brain works, let's understand money and abundance, I began studying in earnest.

At a conscious level, my mind perfectly understood the teachings of Abraham Hicks, of Denise Duffield Thomas, of Tony Robbins, of Napoleon Hill, of Robert and Kim Kyosaki, of Wallace D Wattles, Darcie Elizabeth, Marianne Williamson, Joanna

Hunter, of every single person on earth who taught the principles of mainstream financial advice and spiritual abundance.

But it was not until I unlocked the spiritual connection to a lack of abundance that my world began to change. It was when I cried "enough!" I cannot work with the conscious mind any longer. There must be a deeper reason that I connected to my true knowledge of reincarnation.

It was a turning point in my life, finally recognising that all the books, courses, and solutions provided by others were not a part of my journey any longer. I needed to take what I had learned and dig deeper. I needed to move into the part of my mind that was eternal. The superconscious mindstream.

My frustration was my key to understanding my break-through. It was showing me where I was not aligned. It showed me that there was something calling me, something that I needed to explore, that would help not only me, but others who were experiencing the same level of dissatisfaction with the traditional teachings on money and the spiritual teachings on abundance and the mainstream teachings of how the mind works.

It was time to throw in the towel and start again, to find my own soul's knowledge on the subject, to dare to think that I had something additional to contribute. And so, I began to ask the question, "Who am I?" And more importantly, "Who have I been, or are being simultaneously, that is impacting my life, by impacting my thoughts and actions that I have no awareness of?"

And so, the journey began, and continues.

For every life that I unlock, I free my mind of the programming that I had personally created in another lifetime. For each vow and limiting belief that I reprogram and reframe, I get another layer of freedom.

This has been the true blessing of my life. To find the answers in the shadows of my soul, and to understand the lessons within. I am disentangling my mind with each breath that I take and helping others to do so as well. This is the definition of freedom.

To learn more about reincarnation and how the mindstream works over all lifetimes, you can listen to my free podcast "The Infinite Life with Katische Haberfield" which is available on all podcast players including Spotify, Apple, Amazon Music and Audible or head to https://the-infinite-life.captivate.fm/ to listen via your browser.

If this chapter sparks a knowing in yourself that there are limiting beliefs to be uncovered and reframed and healed at the level of the superconscious mind, please contact me for a session at katische.com and complete the application form. It would be my honour to assist you.

About the Author

Katische Haberfield helps old souls, starseeds, and light-workers to break free of karmic behaviours and limiting beliefs impacting their potential and soul purpose. She accesses the sub- and superconscious mind across all lifetimes to tap into and break the patterns, beliefs, and karmic vows that are holding you back, so you can live a life according to your soul's desires – not your ego or your karmic past.

Sessions with Katische are bespoke and incorporate many of her modalities (including age and past life regression, life between lives regression, future life progression and akashic records healing) according to your needs. She has a passion for helping people with abundance of all levels (especially financial and relationship) and unlocking the most important kind of abundance – an abundance of self-love.

She is a psychic, a medium, and a profound healer with sound and light at the fourth-dimensional level, where she works with Saint Germain, Yeshua, and other members of her animal, interplanetary, and spiritual team. When she's not working,

ENTANGLED NO MORE

Katische loves sharing the light through photography, hiking in nature, and chasing around her beloved teenage sons in her mum's taxi. To connect with Katische, please visit:

https://www.katische.com

KRISTINE McPEAK

Self-Blooming

Audrey Hepburn's words, "to plant a garden is to believe in tomorrow," have new meaning in my life. *Life*. What a powerful word, these four mighty letters. I often wonder how I've made it, alive, this far. I was nearly smothered by my own thoughts and behaviors. At one point, I was almost strangled.

It is still a mystery – and truly a miracle – that I didn't suffocate in my 20's, tangled up by my own insecurities, bound up by one poor choice after another. I haven't died yet, and somehow, I've managed to survive. However, it just wasn't in my tool kit to learn how, much less to consider, that I could begin to *thrive*. I needed to learn how to nurture myself by putting self-love into action.

The dictionary defines the word "thrive" as "growing vigorously, flourishing, gaining wealth or possessions, prospering." I didn't feel any of these things. Instead, survival had been my brain's only priority. There were many close calls, potentially leading to death knocking at my unruly and untended garden gate. I only started to learn how to grow and thrive in my fifth decade.

Even at an early age, I was confronted with death. I nearly drowned in a lake when I was four years old. As I no longer struggled to tread water, nearly succumbing to the peaceful light shining from above, the strong grip of a stranger yanked me to the surface. I was safely on shore. Cold, limp, and alive. Yet to live another day. And on another hot and hazy day, I hesitantly dipped my toes back in the water. I began to splash and eventually swam again! I never realized that my lifetime would be filled with overcoming and facing so many of my fears. Ironically, I would spend many days trying to rescue strangers from drowning in their own misery.

As a teenager, I desperately wanted to leave the planet. The darkness was too dark. I had begun to hate myself. I didn't feel that I'd been living up to who I thought I was supposed to be and believed that I'd let my family down. I was the black sheep. Bringing shame to our family name by getting arrested for marijuana, and for shoplifting. I had brought embarrassment to my household by sneaking out to parties, skipping school, and for being defiant and disobedient.

Many summers later, mesmerized by the same lake that nearly took my life a decade earlier, my grandmother, Faith, and I had a life-changing conversation. "How *could* he do that to her?" I snapped to attention, curious about who she was talking to, or about. I never knew I would spend a lifetime listening to people vent. As she mumbled the words under her breath, "he was foolish, and selfish!" I heard the frustration beneath her closely guarded anger. A young man had completed suicide. I also heard her sense of helplessness as she spoke about her friend's pain, the young man's grandmother. In that pivotal moment, near where my father's ashes would later be scattered, I decided that I would never cause Faith the same pain, by ending *my* life.

And that day on the bench, while I chose to not end my life, I also did not deal with the pain that I was feeling. Instead, I spent another decade or three running from my internal turmoil and distracting myself with unhealthy relationships with food, and people. I learned how to temporarily escape by numbing my pain with alcohol or marijuana, sometimes sprinkled with cocaine or LSD. So many hours, so many brain cells wasted. So many moments believing my own untrue thoughts. "Nobody likes you!" And, I believed the harsh words of others, "you're always SO mean!"

By consciously and unconsciously choosing unhealthy relationships, I wasn't cultivating a positive, fertile environment to entertain this foreign concept of *thriving*. Heck, I was barely surviving. I didn't know how to self-regulate or soothe my savage thoughts. I did not know the Latin name for my Grandmother's favorite flower, *Convallaria majalis*, nor did I have a clue how to feel calm. And I didn't know how to muster up the sweet, soothing scent of the delicate and fragrant Lily of the Valley to help regulate my mind. I wish I had these tools as a teenager, that I had learned to be more aware of my thoughts, more mindful of my breathing. "Breathe in, breathe out, as if smelling grandma's flowers." Much later in my life, I would repeat this mantra many times. I had little sweetness, no budding Lilies of the Valley, and definitely no fruition for much of my life.

I did inherit a few things from my grandmother – her smile, her love of flowers and her witty and sarcastic tongue. The Latin root of sarcasm points to a "dog tearing at flesh." I learned to wield sarcasm to protect myself from being hurt by another. I could hurt others before they could hurt me. Even armed with this weapon, I was still unstable, at best, and I was barely treading water.

During a lifelong period of emotional drought, it looked like the rest of my course would head down a very hardened path. When I was 25 years old, my father died from a rare, cancerous brain tumor that attacked his mind, but did not steal his brilliant wit and humor – two precious gifts he left for me. Things finally started to change when I started doing things to earn his respect posthumously. I became a Big Sister volunteer because he volunteered with this organization. His death gave me a new sense of purpose, to make him proud, by living my life fully. He died just before finals week, and somehow, I completed that last semester of college. I started to feel stable for the first time, and I began to see a counselor. Yet, the changes were short lived, as his death ultimately shook me to my core. He had been my rock, my anchor, the tallest sunflower rising above all others. He was uprooted from my life, and he was no longer available to help me laugh or see the bright positives in life's darkness – the sides I had been desperately avoiding. I had learned the hard way that life is messy, stinky, and complicated – like my grandmother's garden compost.

It would take a few more decades to realize, I was emotionally immature, much like a frustrated five-year-old on a bad day or a know-it-all 15-year-old on a particularly sullen day. Nowhere near maturity, merely pretending to be an adult at 25. I was entangled and tortured by my own pain that could no longer be contained. My pain saturated in domestic violence and sorrow. At the time of my father's death, I lived with a man who was medicating his pain with alcohol. His anger was carefully hidden, masked behind his charming smile, and after my front tooth was knocked out, I finally left. Though, I still believed the mantra, "nobody likes you." I didn't like myself much.

Shame kept me from confessing to my dying dad that my life was so messy. And the dam burst when he died. A tsunami, and nothing could hold back the tears that were unleashed, the tears that would penetrate and soften the hard soil of my mind. Anger also erupted from all of my pores, another inheritance, perhaps? I thought I was adept in being able to control all of my messy feelings. I had learned to avoid difficult and uncomfortable topics or conversations. However, anger like unchecked weeds can be insidious in a garden as they creep in and strangle growth. I was not containing the messy thoughts or feelings. And while I had honed my sarcastic edge, my pruning tools were dull.

On the day of my father's memorial service, our family learned there had been a radio tribute playing his favorite songs, honoring his volunteerism. Our stepmother waited to inform us, after it had aired. We were eventually able to listen to the tribute after writing the program director for a cassette copy. To add more salt to the wounds, the original invitation to speak was revoked, much to my surprise, as our stepmother intentionally excluded me from sharing my thoughts. I was omitted at the last minute from the formal program. I felt overlooked, insignificant, and a fury was growing deep inside me, while sitting in the pew. My mom encouraged me, at the end of the program, to stand in line with people who wanted to share their stories. I just wanted to run as fast and as far away as I could, to the top of a mountain to scream at the top of my angry lungs. Instead, quietly fuming, I stood in the long line, waiting my turn to share, growing more nervous and more irritated. "Damn you for keeping us from our dad while he was dying, and damn you for dying, Dad!" Thankfully, I didn't voice any of my thorny thoughts from the pulpit!

As I somehow managed to read my carefully prepared words, through the tears, the omission was now painfully evident to the minister. "I'm sorry, I didn't realize Mike had two other children", his gentle eyes penetrating mine after the program, and I somehow smiled, sniffed, and said, "thank you". Looking back, that day was a blur of tears, snot, and only a few memories stand out clearly. It was a day mixed with overly concerned looks, with snotty tissues and empty tissue boxes, with hesitant hugs, and it was a day consumed by my constant thoughts wondering when I could leave to get high. Wondering when the nightmare would end. I still desperately wanted my life to end.

Even still, my mind, or my ego wanted to appear composed, containing these messy thoughts and emotions, for other people's comfort. People inquired about my life, exchanging pleasantries while awkwardly avoiding my tired, bloodshot eyes. The concern and compassion were more than I could bear while my heart was breaking. I didn't feel that I deserved their kindness. Somehow, my fruitless life was FINALLY being watered, from the release of pent-up tears, anguish, and self-loathing. The tears began to flow until finally, they could no longer be contained. This day began a journey making friends with my tears, releasing, and granting pardon, allowing my messy emotions their freedom.

Somehow, small miracles occurred in my life. During this tumultuous time, I completed my Bachelor's degree in Education, while secretly living behind the closed doors of domestic violence. I would keep the curtains closed, so my shame and addictions, our anger and our yelling were hidden from the world. Finally, I left, and transplanted myself, by removing myself from this violent relationship and environment in which I was living. And my ongoing dental repair began. A year later, my counselor would suggest that I continue to journal and explore some of my interests, such as past lives, astrology, nature, and flowers. "Explore them", she said, "even if others think it's weird". I never did tell her that I was still entertaining thoughts to end my life.

There is not much I remember from those sessions thirty years ago. Truthfully, I was probably stoned at every one of them. I journaled for a short time, and then I stopped for ten or more messy years. I did pursue some new interests and became curious in learning how our mind works. Fascinated by the beautiful resilience of the brain, I learned as much as I could about the mind, body, and spirit connection. Yet, I still did not realize that my learning and studying had become another distraction, to avoid feeling anything.

I never could have anticipated that a massage class would point me in a focused direction towards feeling, towards releasing and the healing arts. I was able to allow my body to begin to feel, to release long stored up tension and emotions on a trusted practitioner's table. My body felt safe to release tears, that seemed to have no apparent cause or reason. Stored up tears. And with each release, I began to feel hesitantly hopeful. I enjoyed this foreign feeling of being calm and relaxed, after each session. And I wanted to feel this way more often.

Out of my new drive to stay alive and to keep my brain distracted from the darkness, I studied and explored many journaling and holistic techniques throughout the years. I began to learn through life's formal and informal studies about more interests: architecture, massage, laughter, chakras, leadership. Those interests then led to more studies: Healing Touch, Emotional Freedom Technique, Health Coaching, Rapid Resolution Therapy.

One class in particular caught my interest as I was always a lover of nature and flowers. I especially enjoyed what I learned in Landscape Architecture 101. And, as I began to grow my own flowers, I found that I could lose myself for an entire afternoon in the dirt. Digging, transplanting, watering, nurturing my plants, and I especially enjoyed fresh flowers in my home. The fruits of my labor were bringing hope into my home and into my life.

While digging in the dirt, I would reflect back and see how life had become my classroom. My garden would become a mirror for life's many lessons. By gardening, I've learned how to plan, how to have patience, how to nurture, and how to identify companion plants. I learned how to identify weeds, which plants needed sunshine and which ones preferred shade, which plants were drought tolerant, and which ones liked extra water. I learned, through gardening, how to believe in the future. I learned that I could get lost sitting in the soil, lost in the moment, watching a bee feast on lavender, losing an entire day digging in the dirt. I felt a sense of timelessness and freedom, instead of feeling trapped by my own thoughts.

Slowly, I began to share what I was learning with others. And at last, I was using my education degree teaching others how laughter could help us change our brain chemistry. I shared that we can trick the brain by noticing our thoughts, and shift our internal dialogue with a deep breath, or pretend to laugh. How a smile could affect our mood. Even when it seemed I was dangerously close to the edge, close to drowning in my own quicksand, stuck in one unhealthy relationship after the other, I learned that I could also be resourceful and helpful. I started dreaming about the future, one helping others.

During the eight years I owned a home, I was able to cultivate beautiful gardens. I was able to begin healing my spirit while doing so. I would spend one Saturday after the next nurturing and caring for plants and, ultimately my soul, in the process. When I sold my home, it became difficult to maintain a perennial garden because I spent almost twenty years living in and out of boxes, moving from place to place. I eventually stopped planting things. I even gave up on houseplants. Somehow, I found myself in my mid-forties, in the midst of yet another unhealthy relationship, with yet another wounded soul. Alcohol, addictions, more violence and mutual anger were at the center of our relationship. I'd stopped dreaming about flowers and gardens, and I'd stopped dreaming about the future. I still had more pruning and more growth ahead of me.

On a dreary day, driving down a desolate dirt road, one lonely sunflower caught my eye. I thought about my dad, and again, how he would not be proud of my life path. I was inspired, and returned to gardening, becoming involved in my neighborhood's Community Garden. Initially, it was a new form of escape. Healthier than numbing out on television or marijuana. It was also time away from home. To clear my head, to think clearly as the domestic violence curtains of shame were still tightly closed. Living in the darkness, once again, I bravely stepped into the sun, engaging my mind, body, and spirit in planning, planting, watering, weeding. I began enjoying the fruits of my labor, and those fresh flowers in my home once again kept me grounded and balanced. Vegetables on my table brought me a new sense of accomplish and confidence.

While in this second significant and equally unhealthy relationship, my pride and shame also kept my mom in the dark. She didn't know how truly dangerous and unhealthy this relationship was and sent me a card with a flower on the front. It read, "a flower has to push through a lot of shit to bloom." She wrote of my resilience. This was a definition I would later look up, "the capacity to recover quickly from difficulties; toughness." I sought out a second counselor. We addressed codependency and anger. From these sessions, as I shared my story, characters began to appear in my journaling. Mean Kristine, the Badger Queen, had only a few friends: a stinky skunk and a lone cat, Mr Lucky Kat. And as I grew stronger internally, I began sharing my story with others, no longer excluding the thorns and the weeds.

It's been quite the experience, this awakening journey, these twisty-turny five and a half decades. Life has mostly been prickly and thorny and is now becoming peaceful and sweet. This path I have been navigating hasn't always had an agreeable fragrance, and it was especially unpleasant during those terrible teen years. Some of my relationships are still affected by that part of my past.

My teenage soul and soil were very messy. Filled with angst and bitterness, seeds were planted. My mind was full of weeds, entangled with negativity and bitterness. My soul was being choked by patterns of thought and behaviors that wouldn't be uprooted for decades. I didn't have the tools to eradicate the effects of trauma, to uproot unappealing and detrimental thoughts. I did not know how to weed or prune my own mind, or how to turn my hardened, toxic soil into fertile potential.

Anger was the most consistent and persistent weed keeping my soil, my mind, and my soul toxic. From teen years to my fifties, frustration followed me. Irritations abounded, and these both can lead to anger. I asked the Universe, I asked God, to please eradicate my explosive anger. It seemed to be an insidious, noxious, and prolific weed.

Thankfully, in a moment of rage, in my forties, I saw my finger pointing at another wounded soul, and I saw that I had three fingers pointing back at me. I don't remember what words I was yelling. And, in a moment of clarity, I do recall this to be the beginning of my journey to make friends with my anger. I had made friends with my tears, and I could befriend anger, too. I learned that anger is an emotional barometer or indicator urging us to take action.

Having read and studied a lot, I knew from my Physical Therapy training that "feel good" messages reach the brain faster than "pain messages." I knew that pain and anger have a close relationship with one another. And I had to learn how to first notice when I was angry, sad, overwhelmed, or frustrated. Noticing, and having awareness was a key that pulled back the curtains to begin to unlock my shadow work. I learned that emotional pain I'd been feeling wasn't much different than physical pain.

I knew from my background and experiences that calming my nervous system down was most important. I could then begin to dig deeper to find the seed, the thought pattern that was driving an emotion or behavior. Now, when I feel anger or another strong emotion creeping in, I begin to gently tap on my collarbones, using Emotional Freedom Technique (EFT) to help calm down my nervous system. I also began to practice breathing techniques, radical self-forgiveness, reframing my thoughts, and shifting my perspective. I learned to sing silly songs to dissipate feelings of anger, and to excuse myself from a conversation or walk away so I could self-regulate.

Previously, I had barely considered how to blossom or thrive. I knew that I was a survivor. I knew that I was tough, or resilient. A new mantra, "I've got this," grew from my mom's card and her words. I trust that my mom now believes that if I cannot tend my internal garden, I would seek counseling for a third time. I trust that she believes in the efficacy of the tools I have acquired in the last three decades since my dad's funeral. I trust that she knows that I am finally thriving internally – more than merely surviving. I trust that she knows my heart still beats to its own weird and wacky rhythm. I trust that she knows that while my voice may shake, I am here, still, to tell silly stories, or lyrics that my dad still gifts me. I trust myself, and I am now beginning to blossom. Having shifted and pushed through a lot of life's messy dirt.

I know I am still here to be of service, to teach others about tools that help foster internal fortitude, resilience. To encourage others to believe that no matter what life dishes us, or what weeds live in our gardens, we can learn to thrive! We can uproot the unhealthy patterns and negative thoughts. We can re-till the soil, reframe, and we can re-plant and water new seeds.

I'm still a work in progress, as all gardens are. My relationship with anger is much healthier. I wouldn't change a thing – not one single experience of my life, not losing a front tooth to domestic violence, not losing my father to cancer, not the emotional abuse from my short marriage, or the domestic violence from two relationships. I would not change sibling estrangement, which is another story for another day.

My soil, my heart, my brain, and my mind are now fertile and clear. I plant seeds of positive thoughts and I pull the weeds or harmful thoughts, leaving room to nurture those which I want to enhance in my life. If I could have written my life story forty years ago, it would be much different than it has unfolded so far. My garden path has eventually led me to develop a strong sense of self-awareness, a passion for learning about healing, and a drive to help and be of service to others.

Most importantly, I am now constructing a strong nurturing pathway of self-care and self-love which leads to a beautiful and unique garden, wild and colorful, fragrant, and varied. I have become a desert flower. I can bloom wherever I am. I now live in a very dry area, and as I watch tumbleweeds roll with the wind, I cannot help but see a similarity in my life. We are planting seeds all the time, whether we're aware or not.

Self-care, self-love, and self-nurturing require actions and sometimes radical action. And sometimes we have to uproot thought patterns or transplant ourselves in order to flourish, to move beyond survival. Some flowers and life lessons smell sweet, and some stink like composting shit. It's up to the gardener to decide if it needs weeding and uprooting or tending and nurturing. While I'm a late bloomer, I'm blossoming now. And right now, is all that matters

Life. I'm shifting perspective daily. I'm glad I'm alive, adding tools to my toolkit, sharing lessons and stories with others. Life is a classroom, a grand adventure, a beautiful garden. And I plan to continue to thrive and to live the rest of my days planting intentional seeds, pruning, weeding, nurturing, learning, blooming, and sharing more with others on how we can all learn to blossom and thrive!

"You can complain because roses have thorns,
or you can rejoice because thorns have roses."
Zig Ziglar

About the Author

Kristine earned her BS in Elementary Education in 1992, though never landing a formal classroom, life became her teacher. Not long after, she became a Certified Laughter Leader through The World Laughter Tour, and began helping others by leading therapeutic laughter groups while sharing the health benefits with friends, businesses, and clients.

After earning another degree in 2012, she found herself working with elders as a Physical Therapist Assistant. She then went on to study Healing Touch, which is a continuing education program. Healing Touch is also an energy modality recognized by the American Holistic Nurses Association, and she is a trained Level 4 Practitioner. When a crisis arose in her life, Kristine learned about Emotional Freedom Technique (EFT). Having personally experienced the effectiveness, she then studied to become an EFT Practitioner and has been sharing this tool with others.

In 2019, she furthered her mind-body-spirit knowledge through the Institute for Integrative Nutrition, becoming a Health Coach. She also became a student of Rapid Resolution Therapy in 2021. Continuing to develop these new skills to help others reframe, shift and release unbeneficial core beliefs, she now helps others become clear and free from lifelong struggles.

As a lifelong learner, Kristine has taught downhill skiing, numerous exercise classes, and facilitated therapeutic rock painting for all ages. Mostly, she loves to incorporate laughter and play into teaching effective tools to others. She finds joy in guiding others to discover and clear troublesome patterns. Kristine helps identify tools that can relieve stress, release trauma, and reframe thinking. Tools that help you experience more inner peace. So you can shine!

Living a life of service, she helps others move toward self-actualization, self-empowerment, and self-love. Personally, she continues her growth, by deeply contemplating the Gene Keys with others around the world.

Kristine (Unique) McPeak is developing a 12-week curriculum based on teachings through her Health Coaching studies, as well as a new class, loosely titled, Self-Kare 111, to be launched in January 2023. Stay tuned for the Adventures of Mr Lucky Kat Tales, a series of easy reader stories that hold timeless lessons, written for kiddos of all ages.

Visit her FaceBook page, PeaceSHINE, or you can find more information on her new website, www.uniquemcpeak.com You can also join her monthly zoom class, (f)ART.ing Around with Friends. There, you will be encouraged to use art in safe and playful ways, as you are gently guided to notice your inner critic.

In the meantime, if you need to quiet your inner critic, or are feeling stuck, reach out to her at kristinemcpeak@gmail.com

LAURA MUIRHEAD

A Funny Thing Happened
on the Way to My Life

How many times have I sat on that couch in my best friend's family room? It was probably hundreds. But that night as I sat there crying, my body shaking, I knew this time was different. There was no going back.

Less than an hour earlier, I left her house to go home that Sunday evening, filled with the joy of having hung out with my friend. Walking into my house, I was confronted by my step-mother, Donna. It was August and the end of what could be considered a turbulent summer.

Only two months earlier I had graduated from high school. I started working at a print shop full time during the day while continuing my part-time job at a grocery store at night. Some days, I would drive straight from my day job to the grocery store, keeping my work clothes in my car, and changing when I got there. At night, I would get off work anywhere from 10 pm to midnight and then return to work in the morning by 8:30 am. I was also trying to balance work with a social life of the seventeen-year-old girl that I was.

Just a couple of weeks earlier, my dad had asked to meet with me. He came home from work in the afternoon to tell me that he and his wife were having marital problems. He went on to say that one of their issues was that my stepmother, Donna, didn't think I loved her. Yes, you read that right. She didn't think that I loved her which was causing *their* problems. Even as a newly graduated high school student at 17 years old, I knew that was one of life's BS excuses.

My dad and stepmother were swinging at anything to avoid their own personal responsibility. A few years later, my sister told me that Dad had a similar meeting with her, but the story he told her was that their marital issues were because his wife was interested in having a relationship with her boss.

Over that summer, Donna frequently complained about my life choices like working two jobs or spending time with friends. I heard over and over that she thought I wasn't home enough.

"You're never home! Why don't you just go live at your friend's house since you're there all the time anyway?" I thought that was ridiculous.

The pressures of life were building up. One Sunday, I arrived at home, and she complained again for what felt like the 8 millionth time, it would be the last. I reached my limit. I'd had enough. I looked straight at her angry face and asked, "Okay. Would you like me to leave right now or in the morning?" She didn't say a word, just stood there with a deer in the headlights look, so I picked up my purse, my car keys, and I left. Luckily, my friend and her family opened their home to me, and I never went back.

In hindsight I know my stepmom had her own unhealed areas and was doing the best she could with what she knew. She had her own problems that were there long before I became her stepdaughter. She was blaming anyone she could for her problems. Her insecurities were compelling her to try to control everything.

Leaving that day may seem spontaneous, and in some sense, it was. But truthfully, I had been longing to leave for years – eight long years, in fact. It all started when I was nine. Before that it was a carefree life of what I thought was a happy middle class, suburban family, while my mom and dad were married. Then one day everything suddenly changed while we sat in the car at a red traffic light. My mom announced to my sister and me that she and my dad were splitting up. And that was it. My parents were getting divorced. In the time it took for the light to turn from red to green my life was changed! My sister would live with Mom, and I would live with Dad. That was the entire conversation. Two sentences. We were a captive audience there in the car. I had no idea on that day how different my life would be in a short amount of time.

At that early age, I didn't even fully know what divorce really meant. I'd heard that word here and there. Was it on a TV show? Not sure. I do remember there was a country song that I had heard: "Our d-i-v-o-r-c-e becomes final today." They couldn't even say it; it had to be spelled out. It definitely couldn't be good.

Just a few weeks before that, life had been fun. I was at the state fairgrounds showing my pony. We didn't actually own the pony. Someone that Mom knew had the pony and offered to let me take care of him. I don't know all the arrangements, but he was moved to the stable where I took riding lessons, and for all intents and purposes, he was mine. I'd never been happier, having a pony of my own to ride was a dream come true. What a character my pony was, though. If you know ponies, then you know what I'm talking about. Ponies can be stubborn. We couldn't ride the whole circumference of the outdoor arena without him heading for the barn. So, we would cut off the circle and ride through the middle. That seemed to help lessen his determination to head home.

Within a week or two of the horse show, I ended up sick. It turned out to be my appendix. The doctors had some trouble determining the exact issue because my appendix was 'in the wrong place.' By the time they operated, I had quite an infection so extensive that the doctors left a tube on one side of the incision so the infection could drain from my body.

School was almost finished for the year. I think I may have only returned for the last half day. When you're nine, time seems to take a long time. Looking back, and not really remembering the exact timing of everything, a lot of life changes happened in a few months.

After the divorce announcement, our house went up for sale. Mom bought a condo. Dad rented a duplex for the two of us to live in. I remember the first day of fourth grade was moving day. My sister was able to stay home that day, but I had to go to school. I couldn't understand why she could stay, and I couldn't. Children in those days were meant to be seen and not heard. "Do as you are told. Don't ask questions." Parents, or at least mine, didn't explain things.

Why were they even getting divorced? It didn't seem like they fought with each other. Why was it decided that I would live with Dad and my sister with Mom? Did Dad lose and was stuck with me? I can remember hiding under my bed. I just wanted to disappear. The living arrangements did actually make some sense though. I was with Dad a lot, helping him wash the car, playing catch in the backyard, or running errands with him.

It was a confusing time. The events that unfolded had certainly not been in my nine-year-old's life plan.

Then the most crushing blow came to my nine-year-old self. I couldn't have my pony anymore. Why? Because we were moving. But he didn't live with us anyway, so it made no sense to me. The pony was still at my stable. Someone else had started riding him. It broke my heart to see him at the stable but now a new girl was riding him. It was torture for me. I couldn't understand it all. Don't ask questions; they aren't allowed. At least, I was still able to take riding lessons... for a few more months.

Sometime over that summer, Dad started spending more and more time with his secretary. You know, doing nice things for her like mowing the lawn and washing her car. In my naive world, I thought he was just being nice and helpful. One time, we went to the beach with her and her two girls. It felt strange and a bit awkward to me. I didn't even know them! Soon enough, we were spending a lot of time with them. They got engaged. On Thanksgiving weekend that year, they were married.

Remember what I said about time seeming to be longer when you're young? What I found out much later in life was that my parents' divorce was final in October, only about a month before my dad remarried.

Now life was really changing. The three of them moved into our two-bedroom duplex. My grandma stayed with us while they went on their honeymoon. Again, it seemed like a while, but looking back, it could have only been a few weeks, then we moved into a new house. And again, life changed. The new house wasn't in my school district, so I went to a different school for the second half of fourth grade. It wasn't the best school for me. I didn't belong there, and I hated it. Finally, my mom realized that it wasn't a good fit and arranged for me to go back to my old school for fifth grade. It must have been apparent that my emotional and mental health was suffering. She may have used that in her negotiations with the school administrators to accomplish the change back to my original school. I know my stepmom didn't like it. She now had to drive me to school every day, and she wasn't happy about it. Regardless, it was a better situation for me.

When I was young, we went to church as a family. It was a Lutheran church in the town where my whole family lived. My grandparents, cousins, aunt and uncle all went there. My cousins and I were in Sunday school together. We moved from that town when I was six, and for whatever reason, we stopped going to church at all.

Well, we were back. After my dad and his new wife were married, we started going to her church, a Christian church. We attended Sunday morning services, vacation bible school, church camp, read bible stories, went to potlucks. We did it all like I heard good Christians do. I did it all… like it or not.

Once we were all moved into the new house and settling in together, there were a few more life changes. No more riding lessons for me. Either we all took riding lessons, or none of us could. Turned out it was none of us. There was a new haircut also. It was the same cut that my stepsisters had. I was instructed to wear dresses to school at least every other day. Girls are supposed to wear dresses, in case you didn't know.

On weekends, I would go to stay with my mom. It wasn't every weekend though. As far as I know, there wasn't an actual schedule. Whenever it worked out, I went. She had a nice two-bedroom condo. Just right for her and my sister. Since I really didn't live there, I didn't have a room of my own. I slept in my mom's bed with her or sometimes on the couch when I was there. My sister's room was decorated to her exact liking. She even let me go in there a few times!

Looking back, it was easy to see I had become a square peg, not quite fitting in my mom's life and not quite fully fitting my dad's new life either.

Anyway, in just over a year, I had surgery and a week-long stay in the hospital, my parents got divorced, they sold our house and moved out of it, Dad got married to someone I barely knew, moved the new wife and kids into the duplex with us, then bought the new house, so we moved again into that house, a new school, and then back to my old school, a new church and a new religion. No more pony or riding lessons. No more dressing or looking like myself. Talk about life changes!

NONE of it was in my nine-year-old self's life plan. Talk about 'a funny thing happened on the way to my life…'

My stepmother, Donna, and I had a rocky relationship from the beginning.

Imagine being told that everything about you needs to change, from the way you wear your hair to your clothes to how you speak or even how you express yourself? And imagine that the person who tells you to change does so daily without a break.

"Girls don't dress like that!"

"Girls don't speak like that!"

"Girls don't like to play catch or wash the car with their dad!"

Then to ice that cake, you are forced to look like your step-sisters and share all your worldly possessions with them. To receive such negative conditioning as a child, you would think it would create an unhappy adult. You would be right.

However, I believe in our inherent individuality, and despite all this conditioning, it is possible to love and respect yourself just as you are and even get back to the person you were always meant to be.

I was able to do just that by making the radical choice of personal responsibility and setting good boundaries and standards, or what I call "personal policies." You might think that the people you grew up with, that you spent eight years of your young life with, would continue to be part of your life as an adult. That isn't the case for me. Even when I was older, the interactions with them were less than pleasant for me.

Despite the outward conditioning that we got from others to accept people because they are family, you don't have to go along with that. I didn't. It's not always easy, but in my experience, the peace that you gain is well worth it. Blood related or not, we deserve to have supportive people that we enjoy in our lives. If there are people, even family members, who don't reach that bar, then they can't ride the ride with you.

At seventeen, I reached my limit and decided to be entangled no more with people who didn't respect my individuality or failed to be supportive. These experiences helped me shape my personal policies that I use to navigate life's curves in the road as they come.

Life is full of plot twists. Throughout my own life, there have been many plot twists, including a house fire, but that is a story for another time. These plot twists have all been both amazing and challenging. I want to share with you my top 5 tips for navigating them:

- **Have personal policies in place.** These are minimum standards that you are willing to accept or not accept. In my world, we call these "the Queen Code." At seventeen, I knew what I was willing to accept or not accept, but you can set your queen code at any age. It's never too late.

- **Follow your dreams.** The dream of riding horses stayed with me. When I was 33, I started taking lessons again. That lead to not only showing horses but also building and owning my own boarding stable. Choose yourself and make your dreams come true.

- **Allow others to help you.** Sometimes we can be our own worst enemy. Even when we don't know what's good for us, if somebody is genuinely trying to help you, let them. I had no idea how much it would mean to me to have a supportive friend to turn to in my moment of need when I left my home at seventeen.

- **Be flexible.** When life doesn't go according to plans, we need to be willing to change. Hanging on to something that isn't working may actually be the thing that is dragging you down. Time to shout, "Plot twist!" and choose something new for yourself. It's going to be okay!

- **Realize that you are stronger than you think you are,** and you'll always be stronger than the plot twists that life contains.

When you hear me say, 'A Funny Thing Happened on the Way to My Life,' know that this was just the beginning. Having my childhood experiences under my belt and knowing that I can always rely on my own personal policies and choose myself has served as a solid foundation to creating a life that works. It has made me passionate about helping others to do the same by creating their own personal policies and live life with more ease, flow, and clarity.

About the Author

Having been called a 'Jack of all trades, Master of None,' Laura Muirhead prefers 'Jill of all trades, Master of Many.' Laura is an artist, healer, sage, and a multi-passionate business owner. As a result of her plethora of experience, she can easily find a common connection with almost anyone.

Laura is passionate about supporting and encouraging others to be successful in their own individuality. She uses universal energy to creatively work with women who are spiritually curious to gently guide them to stand in the power of their personal policies, find what makes them happy, help them express their true authentic selves, and reclaim the keys to their queendom for a life that is their happy place.

Laura spends her time split between owning and running a family business with her husband in New Jersey and her pottery and art studio located in Michigan. She is the host of the A Funny Thing Happened on the Way to My Life® podcast, and author of a children's book as well as a collection of personal growth journals.

Website: https://www.lauramuirhead.com

Podcast: https://bit.ly/AFTBZ

Instagram:https://www.Instagram.com/laura_muirhead_

LISA PHILLIPS

You Can't Polish a Turd

It took me over seven painful attempts to get out and stay out of my five-year verbally and emotionally abusive relationship. Every day that I chose to stay, I kissed goodbye to my sparkle, my dignity, my self-respect, and most of all, my self-esteem.

Within these five years, my identity departed down the plughole, and emotionally, I was a downright wreck. Looking back, I am still bewildered to recall how sneakily the abuse seized hold of me. That is the thing with emotional abuse, it is often not obvious at first but tends to just creep up on you like being boiled alive very slowly. It's not that you wake up one morning to discover that your self-esteem has been stolen – it just sort of gets chipped away, bit by bit, with every harsh word or unpleasant encounter. Then, before you know it, your self-esteem and confidence seem to have gradually eroded into a big black hole leaving you feeling depleted and helpless.

Prior to meeting my (now ex) partner, I was a sane 30 something who smiled and giggled a lot. Although originally from the UK, I had moved to Sydney, Australia, held down a very successful managerial position, and my life seemed to be ticking along rather nicely. I had great friends, travelled extensively, and life was on the up – or so I thought.

Then, one momentous day, along came my very own personal 'charming' abuser who sucked the life out of me and swept me away into an existence stuffed with heartache, tears, and craziness. I was so desperate to be loved that I ignored all the red flags. Twelve months in, I was a nervous wreck teetering on eggshells, prone to random eruptions of anxiety and anger. I had completely lost who I was.

In the space of a twelve-hour day, I estimate that I squandered six hours formulating cunning new game plans to gain his love and approval, five hours trying to change my own behaviour to prevent me from inadvertently doing something to agitate him, and 60 minutes trying to convince myself that it would be better for me to leg it out of this relationship.

I also tried every trick in the book to get my partner to spot the error of his ways and treat me like a normal human being. Needless to say, after what was probably thousands of imaginative attempts, it didn't work – but hey, I kept clinging onto the dream that maybe, just maybe, I may uncover the illusive magic potion to transform him from a crusty toad into my handsome prince.

My friends thought I was mad, and I felt like I was crazy. It was my unshakeable belief that I was publicly worthless and ugly - oh, and I also felt convinced that nobody, apart from my partner, would ever consider dating me. To put it in a nutshell, I believed I was fatally flawed, and a full-blown relationship reject.

The Light Bulb Moment

Thankfully, one afternoon, a friend spotted that I was about to curl up in yet another ball of depression, waved her magic wand, and dragged me out for a dose of girlfriend therapy. It was on this day that I met Sarah whose words changed my life.

Sarah had been announcing to our group of friends that she had decided to end her relationship with her long-term partner, John. She explained that 'He informed me that he only loves me 90% – That isn't good enough for me, so I told him that the relationship was over. I will only accept 100% positive, fulfilling love.'

Wow! Those words smacked me right in the heart! This was powerful thinking, and there was no way that Sarah would settle for less than she deserved. At this point, I realised that I too wanted to turn my back on situations and relationships where I was being fed leftover moldy crumbs rather than being wined and dined on the full scrumptious chocolate biscuit. I wanted to prize myself enough that I was able to make choices for me which allowed me to honour, respect, protect, and most of all, take extremely good care of myself.

At last, the epiphany had arrived! I had to quit depositing all my energy and hard work into saving a relationship which left me feeling exhausted and tormented. I needed to reclaim my life back and take responsibility for my own happiness. I had to cease putting my life on hold, hanging in there for the imaginary day where my partner would magically metamorphose into the caring and loving man that I always longed for him to be. I had to bail out from planet second best!

Summoning up every last miniscule of courage I had, I made one of the most momentous decisions of my life: I WAS NOT GOING TO TAKE IT ANYMORE!

I knuckled down on my inner work to rehabilitate my life and my self-esteem. The plan of attack for my journey was simple. It was all about ME. I was the common denominator in all my experiences.

I realised that if I wanted to learn to love myself enough that I would only accept nourishing, healthy relationships into my life, then it was up to me to heal. This meant totally giving up on my partner ever changing and quitting analysing why he behaved like he does. My focus had to change from him to the inner ME!

I am not saying that this journey was simple but breaking down some of my own relationship beliefs and patterns was a lot easier than staying in an abusive relationship. Abuse wasn't new to me; it was actually a familiar pattern that had infected my life.

When I began the dig into what was stashed away in my belief system, I was shocked to find out what I really thought of myself. Oh, I could say intellectually that I was an okay person, worthy of the good stuff in life and deserving of meeting Mr. Wonderful, but did I REALLY believe it deep down inside? Not a chance. Like a good girl, I was doing all the right things to prove to the world what a likeable girl I was, flashing my biggest smile to encourage people to approve of me and pretending everything was just fine and dandy, but what was actually fermenting away inside my mind was a completely different story.

The truth was that I was spending each day battling with the familiar flood of critical thoughts which had abducted my mind. I was comparing myself to others, feeling inferior, inadequate, and consistently worrying about what people thought of me. I thought I was ugly, unlovable, and inferior to every other living thing on the planet. Much of my inner dialogue revolved around bashing myself up for not being pretty, successful, slim, brave, or desirable enough. No wonder I accepted crappy relationships!

If that wasn't distressing enough, I had more rage and resentment brimming in my body than a Witches Spell party. Most of it was directed towards my partner for consistently failing to bestow on me the relationship I longed for, persistently letting me down, and generally treating me as if my whole existence, emotions, and happiness were less important than deciding which pair of black socks to wear each day.

What I hadn't sunk into my head at the time was that his behaviour towards me was purely a copy of the exact same behaviour I was directing towards myself. The truth of the matter was that by repeatedly accepting abusive treatment and imprisoning myself in this stinky relationship, I was abusing myself! Not only was I letting myself down by failing to care for and cherish my own emotional wellbeing, but I was behaving as if my entire existence, hopes, dreams, and happiness did not matter one teeny weenie bit!

What we experience in life is always a mirror, so I was being shown an exact copy of my own beliefs, thoughts, and feelings.

A Happy Ending

The good news is that once I had completed the messy inner work, it was so much easier to walk away from this relationship. What is important is being able to leave emotionally, not just physically. If you don't do the inner work first, the chances are you will just find yourself continuing the same pattern. Once I loved and respected myself, I no longer felt willing to tolerate unhealthy relationships. I was free at last.

Every day, I felt stronger and less willing to have people in my life who left me feeling like I was losing my marbles. Each day, it became easier to practice self-care, set boundaries, and be assertive.

Leaving my partner was one of the most courageous and scary things I ever did. I can assure you it is worth it. It is worth living a life where you are free to be yourself, and you don't have to live in fear of the next explosion.

The upshot is that I now feel wonderful and far more content in my life than I ever dreamed was possible. I have re-claimed my sparkle and have waved a terminal 'adieu' to abuse, leaving it fastened securely in my past.

Abuse isn't rare, and it can happen to anyone. Seriously, I take my hat off to people who are in an abusive relationship as they are really some of the most courageous people I have ever met. They are not weak or cowards (as society may think), but they are just like you or me.

A recent survey showed that at least 1 in 3 adults have been abused within an intimate relationship – now that is scary! Thankfully, I can now assist other abusive relationship sufferers to recognize the destructive behaviours of their partner and to find the strength of will to say, 'No more!' Yes, it can take time, but it is one of the joys of my work. Loving yourself is simple, and it can change everything about your life. When you love yourself, you will never settle for second best or keep yourself in a situation which is harmful for you.

Although this relationship was extremely painful, it enabled great clarity and internal healing to take place. The relief I felt in my body and mind after finally leaving, not just physically but emotionally, was transformational. Now, with over 2O years of professional and international experience, I am a qualified counsellor and a Leading Life Coach specialising in assisting people to heal their emotions and really feel good about who they are. I use a wide range of techniques in my practice including inner child therapy, root cause therapy, and somatic healing. In 2015, my book 'The Confidence Coach' was published by Exile Publishing and is recommended reading for several confidence and self-esteem initiatives. I have also won several international awards for my leading-edge coaching techniques and am the current Confidence expert on The Love Destination TV series.

One of my passions is public speaking and I am fortunate to be engaged by several international cruise lines as an enrichment speaker as well as being a popular TV Confidence presenter and wellness speaker.

Since leaving this relationship, my life and career have gone from strength to strength. If you would like to receive my blog, find out about more about face to face, group or online coaching, or book me to speak at your event, please reach out to me at https://www.amazingcoaching.co.uk

About the Author

Originally from Sydney, Australia, Lisa Phillips is an award-winning Life Coach, Confidence Coach, author, and public speaker regularly featured on the TV and radio. Lisa is also the author of 'The Confidence Coach' book (Exile 2015) which is recommended reading for several international self-esteem initiatives. Lisa is also the Confidence and Life Coaching expert on 'The Love Destination' app.

Now based in the UK, Lisa is an extremely popular wellness speaker and is frequently engaged as an enrichment speaker for several international cruise lines: https://www.amazingcoaching.co.uk

LOUISE SQUIRES

The Scapegoat Escaped

As a child, I never went without material things, so to the outside world, my upbringing was considered 'normal.' Growing up with a controlling parent had a big impact on my adult life. I struggled to form friendships, as I was constantly told that my school friends were bad, and I wasn't to spend time with them.

I remember that around the age of 8, I was dropped off at one of my best friend's houses for a birthday party empty-handed. Five of us had been invited to the party, and my friend's mom was taking us swimming. I was the last to arrive, as the door opened, they were all there waiting for me. I noticed everyone was looking down at my hands, expecting to see a card and a present, and I didn't have one. I felt this surge of embarrassment as I realised, and I quickly made the excuse that I had forgotten her present in the rush and would bring it to school. The present never materialised. When I asked if we could go and buy something for my friend to take into school on Monday, I was told, "I'm not buying her anything."

Looking back, this was a common theme throughout my childhood. I can't help but wonder if these things were done on purpose to cause friction with my friends. There was another occasion where I had lent a computer game to one of my friends when I was 12. My mom found out and, instead of allowing me to ask my friend the following day to bring the game back to school, she drove me to her house, sat in the car, and ordered me to go and ask for it back there and then.

School, the following day, was difficult. My friend had told everyone what had happened. Twelve-year-old girls can be nasty at the best of times, but this incident gave them plenty of ammunition. This was a pattern that continued throughout my years at school and into my early twenties.

At the age of 21, I bought my own place, which gave me a degree of freedom. It was during this time that I met my ex-husband. I was in a club, and this older guy approached me and started talking to me. He seemed very friendly and really took an interest in me. Having spent most of my life being extremely shy and quiet, I enjoyed the attention, and we swapped numbers.

Although he was in Birmingham on the night I met him, he didn't live locally. In fact, he lived over 100 miles away in Liverpool. He was working at Birmingham University for a short period of time and was due to go back home in a couple of weeks. I met him again whilst he was still in Birmingham and he explained that he was divorced with three children, and he was 17 years older than me. We really seemed to hit it off, he was very attentive, made plans for our dates and I really enjoyed spending time with him.

When it was time for him to go back to Liverpool, we stayed in touch, and I went up to visit him quite often, which gradually became every weekend. I knew that my mother would not be happy that I had met somebody much older than me with children. I kept the relationship a secret for 18 months, which was quite difficult. She would often call my home phone number in the evenings, and if I wasn't there, she'd then call my mobile number to find out where I was. Although I was 22 at the time with my own house and mortgage, I was being treated like a child. My mother's control over me never went away. The furniture, the decoration, the layout of my home was all determined by my mom and her opinions even though I paid for it all. I went along with it all, as it was all I'd ever known and always had this underlying need to please her.

It was becoming increasingly difficult to keep the relationship a secret, so one day I decided that I would just tell her. At that age, it was one of the most difficult things I had ever had to do.

You would think that telling your mom that you had met someone and that you were happy would be a really joyous occasion.

I took a deep breath and explained to her that I was in a relationship with a man 17 years older than me with three children and that I had kept this a secret from her because I knew how she would react. The reaction was exactly what I expected. She was raging, asking me if I was out of my mind. At the time, we were running a beauty salon together. It was a particularly busy day in the salon, and I had decided that morning to break this news to her. In her rage, she left me there to deal with a day of clients with no explanation as to where she had gone or when she would be back.

The following day, she came into work. The atmosphere was very frosty. I felt relieved that I had revealed the relationship to her, but on the other hand, I felt that I had disappointed her and let her down. After a lifetime of feeling that I needed to please her, it was very difficult for me to cope with her disappointment. Every single day, I was told that I was making a big mistake, then the physical abuse started. Unable to contain her anger with me, she started to push me and slap me. One day, one incident changed everything. We had just finished the day of work in the salon, and she started to shout at me. It wasn't about the relationship; it was something to do with some equipment that had not been put away correctly. But I knew, it wasn't really about the equipment. The anger escalated to the point where I was cowering on the floor, and she was kicking me. I just covered my head and waited for it to stop, until eventually she just walked off and went home.

It was at that moment that I decided enough was enough. I was 23 years of age, and I was not going to live my life this way any longer. I called John and explained to him what happened, and he was horrified. He said, 'Just come and live with me. I'll look after you.' If you're expecting this is where the happy ending is, unfortunately, it's not.

I packed up most of my belongings and made my way to Liverpool. I didn't even think about how I would pay the mortgage or even what would happen to the house I had left behind. I needed to break free of that lifetime of control, and this was a fresh start. The first couple of days living with John were great. I had escaped and finally felt free. That black cloud was hanging over me every single day.

As I was a trained graphic designer, I started to do some freelance work. Work was slow at first. There was income, but it was not enough to cover the mortgage and the bills in the house I had left behind. One day, John came home from work, and I had been doing some graphic design work in the house that day. He had a very angry expression on his face when I saw him in the kitchen. 'Is there something wrong with you?' he said.

'No, what do you mean?' I replied, totally confused.

'This bin absolutely stinks, and you have been sat in this house all day! You're disgusting! How could you be in the house all day and not even think to empty it?'

I quickly went to take the bin bag out of the bin to put it outside.

'Don't bother. I'll do it!' he snapped.

I was very tearful and apologetic. This was the first time I had ever seen him react like this. After a few hours of complete silence from him, he said he wanted to talk. He said I needed to be more thoughtful about his feelings and ensure the house was clean and tidy when he arrived home. He also needed me to start contributing financially to the household. At the age of 23, I didn't see the red flags. I just assumed I hadn't been thoughtful, and I'd done something wrong. It was a reaction I had encountered throughout my childhood from my mom, so it didn't seem unusual to me. I resolved to take on as much work as I could and paid all of my earnings into his bank account.

Within a year, I had built my business into a thriving graphic design and print shop. It was the first time in my life that I could recognise that I was actually good at something. I'd built the business from nothing, gaining new customers by cold calling and arranging meetings to pitch my services.

Seeing the money rolling in, John was living the dream. He had a debit card for my business account and would often go out on spending sprees, clothes, golf, etc. This is when my panic attacks started.

I had a meeting with my accountant, and he asked me to collate all of the receipts for the business expenses. He was looking through the bank statement and asking me about large cash withdrawals that were being made regularly. I didn't even know where the money had been spent. I asked John if he could find the receipts for the things, he had bought from the business account. He instantly went on the defensive and shouted, 'You don't trust me! Why do you need to see receipts?'

I explained that the accountant had asked as it was all in a mess, and he needed records of everything to be able to submit my tax return. 'He doesn't know what he's talking about!' (He used to say this about most people he met).

I felt like I had no control over what was happening. Legally, everything was in my name, and I was ultimately responsible for the accounting and tax. I felt this pain in my chest. I was hyperventilating with a tingling sensation in my arms and hands. I was crying uncontrollably, and I felt like something seriously awful was happening to me. This was a pattern that continued for the next 9 years.

I have heard people say so often when they hear of these relationships: "Why don't you just leave?" It really is not that simple. Narcissistic abusers do not behave in this way 24/7. They can be kind and pleasant for days and then a comment or observation comes out of nowhere. This abuse also builds gradually over months and years, so you're conditioned to feel as though it's normal.

Narcissistic abusers also 'gaslight' their victims. Often, a comment would upset me, and he would say, "I didn't say that" or "You're just being over-sensitive." I would second guess myself all of the time, thinking, "Is it me that is in the wrong?"

Leaving a mentally abusive relationship is extremely difficult. Narcissists need to be in control. If you're leaving the relationship, and it's not on their terms, be prepared for a difficult battle.

After thirteen years in the relationship, we were married, and we had a three-year-old son. John was spending more and more time out of the house. Every evening, he would leave to play golf. I was unhappy, stressed, constantly worrying about finances, and I knew he wasn't out playing golf in the dark. I had just got to the point where I didn't care what he was doing or who he was doing it with.

One weekend, he had said he was working overnight, which is something that he never did, as his hours were 9 to 5. I just knew intuitively that he was somewhere else. On Monday morning, he went off to work, and I logged into his iPad (which was linked to his phone). I could see his work emails, and he had been exchanging explicit messages with a woman in his office. I also could see on his Facebook messages that he was out in town with her on the Saturday night when he had told me that he was working. Around 18 months prior to this, he had told me during an argument that he was going to have an affair with this woman as she fancied him. This was just one of his many attempts to chip away at my self-esteem.

In usual circumstances, discovering that your husband had been cheating would be devastating. I didn't feel devastated. I felt free! This was my reason to leave. He couldn't gaslight his way out of this. The evidence was all there in plain sight.

I sent him a message with a screenshot of one of his messages. He called me instantly, shouting and screaming at me and said he was coming home. Within 20 minutes, he was home saying, "What the hell do you think you're doing?"

I calmly said, "I know you've been lying to me. I'm leaving you. Our marriage is over."

I packed mine and my son's clothes and left that night. The only place I could go to was my parent's house where I stayed for 12 weeks until I found my own place. Those 12 weeks were extremely difficult. John kept turning up at the house trying to speak to me. When that failed, he tried to speak to my parents. He would call my phone over and over again, sometimes 50-100 times a night. He told me he wouldn't allow this break up to happen, and he was going to make my life a misery. He would follow me in his car in an attempt to talk to me. He said I was ruining our son's life by breaking up the family, and I would live to regret it.

I remained strong, although it was extremely difficult. I still had to maintain contact so he could see our son. I had read some articles about narcissist abuse and the advice was the 'grey rock method' which is acting as unresponsive as possible during interactions, avoiding eye contact, and not showing any emotions during a conversation. This helped me to avoid getting drawn into any conversations or arguments, and it became easier the more I did it.

I moved into my new place with my son and finally felt that I was moving away from the toxicity that had surrounded me for most of my life. I vowed that I would not get involved in a relationship like that ever again and was quite happy to remain single for a long time.

Three weeks after moving into my new place, I met Chris. I knew very quickly that Chris was as far away from the toxicity I had experienced as he possibly could be. He faced a lot of hassle from John, following him and confronting him. I did worry that Chris would decide that it was too much and walk away, but he didn't. Eight years later, we are still together, and we have a five-year-old son.

Chris has helped me to understand how a relationship should be. He's supportive, kind, always has my back, and he's an amazing dad to our son. I am so grateful for my lovely family. Both of my boys are so intelligent and determined, and they make me proud every day.

During the Pandemic in 2020, I was facing redundancy from my job in sales, and I had an opportunity to think about what I could do if I was to lose my job. I had worked in sales for nearly 20 years, and I just didn't have a passion for it any longer. It was incredibly stressful trying to juggle a full-time job and two young children and travelling around the country for meetings and conferences.

My passion is to help people, and with the experience from my past, I knew I wanted to help people with anxiety, trauma,

PTSD, phobias, and depression. I did some research and enrolled on an NLP course online during lockdown. I wanted to take the training further and definitely wanted some in-person training, so I found Solution Focused Hypnotherapy.

I signed up for the in-person training which began later that year. In the meantime, I survived the redundancies and was promoted to Area Sales Manager in my full-time job.

As soon as my hypnotherapy training began, I knew it was my calling, I was completely absorbed in every module of the training, which continued for ten months.

I qualified and started to advertise for clients, and I was working evenings and weekends around my full-time job, which was challenging at the time. I found that my clients were making such amazing progress. After a few sessions, they were feeling and coping so much better. They started to refer people they knew to me, and within two months, I had enough clients to go full-time into my hypnotherapy practice.

I made the difficult decision to leave my job. Being qualified as a psychotherapist and hypnotherapist taught me a lot about mindset and limiting beliefs. I made the commitment to myself, and I'm so glad I did!

I now run a very busy hypnotherapy practice in Bromsgrove, in Worcestershire. I see clients face to face, and I also have clients globally, thanks to the ability to be able to conduct sessions online. I see so many people that have been through toxic relationships in many areas of their lives. I use a solution-focused approach which means we do not unpick the past.

I offer my clients a free initial consultation which is an opportunity for them to explain what's been happening, and this helps me to understand. After that, we do not revisit the trauma in any detail. We focus on how my client would like their life to be. I help my clients to set small goals and focus on their strengths. I help them build confidence, resilience, strength, and determination. I help them to understand that they can move on from the damage caused by toxic abuse. They find that inner confidence and become the best version of themselves.

I absolutely love my job! Every day, I see clients doing amazing things, and I feel so proud of them. I have also launched a self-help app which is packed with hypnotherapy sessions, guided meditation, yoga, eBooks for mental health and wellbeing and workshops. This is ideal for people that have not experienced hypnotherapy before and would like to try it, without committing to an appointment. It's also ideal for people that are struggling to find time to make an appointment, as they can use it in their own time, in the comfort of their own home.

Louise Squires – Clinical Hypnotherapist HPD, DSFH, MNCH (Reg.) AfSFH (Reg.), MHS (Reg.)

My website: https://www.louisesquires.com
Email: info@limitless-hypnotherapy.co.uk

My App is available on the App Store and is called Limitless Hypnotherapy. You can download for Apple here: https://apps.apple.com/us/app/limitless-hypnother-apy/id1633955532?uo=4

And Android: https://play.google.com/store/apps/de-tails?id=com.limitless_hypnotherapy.app

About the Author

Louise Squires is a Clinical Hypnotherapist and Psycho-therapist, specialising in helping people with trauma, confidence issues, anxiety, stress, and many other issues. Louise has experienced many toxic relationships in her life, including family, relationships, and work colleagues, which resulted in her suffering with debilitating anxiety and imposter syndrome.

She completely turned her life around through Solution-Focused Hypnotherapy and has worked with hundreds of clients to help them gain in confidence, resilience, and self-belief.

Louise runs a busy hypnotherapy practice based in the UK, where she works one-on-one with clients both online and in-person. She also has launched a self-help app which includes hypnotherapy sessions, guided meditation, yoga, eBooks and workshops. The Limitless Hypnotherapy app is now available on Google Play and the Apple App Store or via her website: https://ww.limitless-hypnotherapy.co.uk You can book a private 121 session with Louise via her website at https://www.louisesquires.com or via her Facebook page, https://www.facebook.com/limitlesshypnotherapyuk

MINA LOVE

Moving on with Love

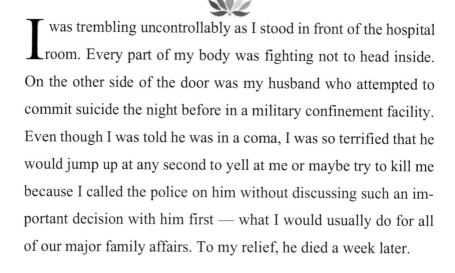

I was trembling uncontrollably as I stood in front of the hospital room. Every part of my body was fighting not to head inside. On the other side of the door was my husband who attempted to commit suicide the night before in a military confinement facility. Even though I was told he was in a coma, I was so terrified that he would jump up at any second to yell at me or maybe try to kill me because I called the police on him without discussing such an important decision with him first — what I would usually do for all of our major family affairs. To my relief, he died a week later.

I never thought I'd end up in this dramatic role that seemed like a scene from a soap opera. I never thought I would ever want to see my husband's face again. I also never thought that I would not be attending my own husband's funeral for I never imagined I would be capable of hating someone so much in my life.

One month earlier, I was having a heated argument with my 11-year-old daughter, Ally.

"I told you to clean your room days ago! Why is your room still a mess? Why won't you just do what I ask you to do when I ask you to do it?!" I screamed at her.

She blurted out, "You don't understand the pain I feel because there is a secret inside of me that is killing me!"

I thought she was just being a Drama Queen as children her age sometimes do, but I was dead wrong. I asked her with a sarcastic tone, "Then tell me what your secret is."

Ally folded her arms across her chest and began to shift her body uncomfortably. She took a deep breath and said, "Dad kissed me." I was shocked and confused. "What do you mean?"

"Dad kissed me on the lips when I was younger. Later, he apologized to me and said that what he did was wrong, but he won't stop."

Everything went silent, even the constant noises of inner judgment, doubts, and fear that usually filled my head. As a survivor of abuse, myself, I knew that the way that I responded to her terrible secret in that moment would have a huge impact on the rest of her life – and mine.

A-ha! So, this is why Ally misbehaves so much! This was the first time I heard the whisper of my heart, a sweet but quiet voice. I didn't want to believe my husband was a monster capable of hurting our own daughter, but the realization of the years of sexual abuse that he committed against our child finally answered the questions that had been puzzling me for years.

For years, I wondered, "Where did Ally learn to lie so well?" and "Why is she acting up constantly?" She would frequently steal things from my room, and then lie to me about stealing with such calm confidence that made me doubt the evidence that I had seen with my own eyes.

She constantly left a mess in her room as if to form a physical barrier to keep us away from her. My heart broke as I realized that she was no longer as close to me as she was as a young child. As the years passed, the emotional gap between me and her seemed to get bigger and bigger. I could never figure out why she was acting the way she was; but at that moment, everything became crystal clear – those behaviors were her way of asking for help and expressing her anger on a subconscious level.

Her honesty about her abuse also explained a few strange inklings that would pop up in my head from time to time. For example, sometimes I would think that my husband looked like the "devil," or I would suddenly feel complete disgust towards him. But since there was no logical evidence for my rational mind, those thoughts would often get brushed aside.

How I wish I knew back then that was my intuition speaking to me and how I wished I never ignored it…

Prior to Ally's confession, my late husband, John, was in the US Navy, stationed in Japan, and I was a photographer. We were a relatively normal family. My husband worked long hours, and I was busy investing time and energy into my new photography business. Like any other mom, I struggled with my tween who had been challenging my authority for years. But overall, I thought we were a pretty "happy" family, in comparison to my own childhood and other stories I've heard before.

I had always been very careful with who I expose my children to. I was fully aware that child perpetrators are often the people closest in a child's life. I myself was molested as a little girl by older children. I just could not believe that my husband, John, who was abused severely by his siblings as a child, would betray my trust and harm our daughter in such a horrific way.

There were no obvious signs of abuse on the surface, so I had no idea how toxic my marriage was until that point in my life. John was well-respected in his career as a dedicated Navy sailor, a dependable provider who helped around the house, and an attentive father. At the time, I was not familiar with narcissistic behaviors and unaware that a charming man can also be a covert abuser. I was ignorant about emotional abuse and the psychological damage caused by long-term gaslighting – all of which I'm still healing from today.

I reported my husband's abuse of my daughter the next day. I was relieved that the investigators were able to bring him in for questioning, and he fully confessed. They kept him in confinement for a few weeks until he attempted to commit suicide. While he was in confinement, I walked around the military base as though nothing was wrong in my life. I simply pretended that John was gone for another deployment. Besides my close friends, no one knew that our world had completely collapsed overnight.

He never recovered from his suicide attempt, and after he passed, I became a widow at the age of thirty-two. My children had lost their father, and I had lost my husband and my home. I was afraid the rumors would hurt my young children, and deep down, I was too ashamed to admit the trauma that had occurred under my own roof as a result of my choice to marry this man.

As a young girl who was often neglected by my emotionally unavailable parents, I felt sad and lonely most of my life. I had a deep fear that my children would be hurt by others as I had been hurt by those close to me. I was terrified that my daughter would leave me like I left my mother. Somehow, I accidentally manifested my own worst nightmare.

I've always been drawn to stories of True Love, but I was confused of what healthy love should be like. The media tends to promote codependent relationships with a strong need for each other's obedience or approval to validate one's self-worth – a very toxic view of love that is well-accepted in our society.

In truth, I had been trying to decide whether I should leave my marriage with John for a while, but underneath my prideful facade, I didn't believe I had enough power to give my children the same lifestyle we had then, so I even considered leaving my children with John, for I believed he was the better parent. (What a horrible idea that was!) It was hard to give up my dream of having a family and my "happily ever after." It was also hard to break free from the years of mental and emotional abuse that I had suffered from my husband which made me dependent on him. I doubted that I would ever be strong enough to be a single mom.

In retrospect, I am so glad that Ally told me the truth when I was at a stage in my life where I started trusting myself more, and I had a group of mom friends who were strong and reliable to help us through. They took care of my children while I dealt with my husband's investigation, fed us when I felt no desire to eat, and got me out of the house when I could not stop imagining the horrible things that happened in our home that was supposed to be our safe place.

Ally's disclosure freed me from my fears of living a life I truly wanted.

That rock bottom was a wake-up call for me to stop seeing the world through a victim lens, especially since it had never helped me before. That life-changing event helped me realize that a part of me knew something that my logical brain did not, and I needed to listen to my intuition. I started experimenting with intuitiveness as if I was playing a game.

I realized that I had trouble trusting my intuition due to my unhealed childhood wounds, fears, and the generational scarcity mindset. Our intuition is like our inner compass. My trauma had caused my compass to malfunction and instead pointed me to my greatest fear (which is a powerful energy). I made so many mistakes as a mom, but my biggest mistake was that I trusted someone else more than myself... I realize now that John's lies and manipulations only worked because I doubted myself so much (something I will never do again).

Four months after I became a widow, my children and I moved to Oregon to start our life anew. I'll never forget the day when I walked into our very first apartment. It was a clear, sunny afternoon with a beautiful blue sky. As soon as we walked into that ground level unit, our eyes were immediately drawn to a large window overlooking three huge pine trees with squirrels running around them. I always felt safe around trees since I was in college, so intuitively I knew those pine trees would help us feel safe while we healed.

Growing up in Taiwan, I was immersed in a lot of beautiful Buddhism and Taoism wisdom, but I also witnessed many people suffering and praying without ever seeing any improvement in their life. I saw many people become superstitious and blindly faithful which made them easy targets for manipulative ill-intended spiritual scammers. So, I chose not to follow any specific type of spiritual practices and instead only followed my own heart and inner wisdom. Whenever I choose a teacher, I check in with their energy and observe if they show up authentically with integrity in their own life.

Since I had never heard of any success stories from talk therapy amongst the people I knew, I did not want to spend years just talking to heal my wounds or waiting a decade to see if it worked for my daughter. I wanted her to have more tools at her disposal. I truly believe children will heal the fastest when immersed in the transformation of their parents, so I invested a lot of time, money, and energy into my own personal development to learn everything about limiting beliefs and other neuroscience tools.

Eventually, I was led back to energy work. Interestingly, the more I learned, the more I realized I already knew and possessed all the tools that I needed. I was intuitively using them for my own healing for years. Everything I learned was more like a confirmation for my logical mind and to unlock my natural ability. No matter what I do, I always check in with my inner being to see if the teachings align with my values and my heart first.

My goal has always been to find the most effective way to help us heal our pain in order to truly move on in life and gain lasting inner peace and joy. My children will only learn how to thrive and be happy in life if they see me demonstrating emotional freedom first. There is no way I can force my children to heal, but I knew they'd follow in my footsteps once they saw me living in bliss. The more I accepted and loved my own imperfections, the more my children started to change, too.

Wherever I traveled on my healing journey, I'd run into women and feel compelled to share my story with them. Many times, these women would thank me for believing my daughter because when they had experienced abuse as a child and shared it with an adult, no one believed them. I didn't need them to thank me, but I understood why they did. It takes a tremendous amount of courage to tell adults things that most people don't talk about. I, for one, did not have that kind of courage when I was a child. I never told my own parents about being molested for fear that they would punish me for lying, or worse, do nothing. The brave women that I encountered reminded me that a mother needs to feel empowered enough to be able to stand up for their children.

I feel heavy-hearted when I think about all the women that I have met in retreats and workshops that are still carrying the wounds of childhood trauma, unable to fully move on. A friend of mine who is a world-famous healer once told me that more than 85% of her female clients had experienced sexual assaults or abuse in their past. Most abuse happened in childhood. I knew that I needed to share my story because I wish more mothers had shared theirs so that I could have had someone to look to in order to process this devastating situation with my daughter. I wish that I had known that abused children sadly often become the perpetrator if they never receive support and help. I desperately wanted to know how some women got to the other side of trauma without closing their hearts.

What started out as a mission for my family became my calling in life: I help empower mothers so they also become emotionally resilient and fulfilled, so they can offer their children a safe home with unconditional love.

There were so many false beliefs I had about my own abilities and what is still possible for us in life to clear out within myself first for me so that one day I can create a sanctuary for other women, where healing is playful, creative, and a beautiful process. Over time, I updated and optimized many traditional healing methods to fit my busy lifestyle as a single mom working at home with two children who also were doing distance learning at home. Courses full of boring homework to journal were triggering for me. Other courses gave concepts that were too vague to be implemented right away. I love how Tony Robbins made personal development so energetic and interesting in his seminars, so I started dreaming of creating my own style of feminine workshops (even though that had to be put on pause as the COVID Pandemic happened).

I call my methods the "Creative Healing Magic Methods," and I use meaningful creative activities to make the process more playful and to help ground the ambiguous knowledge in personal development and the mysterious concepts in the spiritual teachings. There was no way I could have survived the chaos of those first six months after Ally's disclosure without my close friends, and that is why I value the importance of creating intimate sacred circles for the moms I am here to help and support.

I feel the divine love strongest in nature more than in any traditional religious building. I use nature to practice getting out of my comfort zone gently by wandering in neighborhood forests in Oregon, practicing mindfulness walking meditation, and rebuilding my ability to let go of control to trust again in the nurturing space amongst the tall, wise trees. I notice many people walking past me, often missing out on the opportunity to tap into something so much more that the forest wants to offer – something powerful that requires us to slow down and become mindful in order to experience.

I knew my workshops and retreats had to be held in nature, but I find Oregon a bit too chilly and rainy for me, so I waited for a sign to tell me where to go next. In 2021, about a year after the shutdowns, I started seeing the signs everywhere – from a chat with a friend, on a page of a book I randomly opened to read on a travel picture of a TV screensaver, multiple times mentioned during a virtual seminar. All signs pointed to Hawai'i – a place I've always wanted to live, a place I know would be the perfect nurturing ground for healing our feminine wounds, a place full of lively healing energy (after all, it is the healing island of Lemuria). Hawai'i is the perfect place where I could share the divine wisdom and healing; I learned from nature with others in my own creative, healing ways.

I was scared to move my family to a place that I had never been in the middle of a pandemic when the State was about to close its borders. I consulted with my heart, and I knew it was something

I'd regret if I didn't proceed, so I took a leap of faith, trusting that this is where we were meant to be. And the result? Our healing has quantum leaped since then. My children are blooming and so much happier, a progress seldom seen among other survivors or in children who have lost a parent. Today, my two children (14 and 8) and I are enjoying every moment that we have with each other while we create our dream life.

For so many years of my life, I felt like I was all alone, misunderstood, abandoned, and unloved, but looking back now, I see how the dots connected together with each person I met and learned from. Each person along my journey helped me to grow into the next level of me. It took so long for me to see through the illusion the world was telling me: that empaths naturally attract narcissists, that I was powerless to things that happened to me, that bad people and horrible things are happening everywhere, and I can do nothing about it.

By going through the darkest time of my life, facing my fears, I finally saw the light I've searched for my whole life. The unconditional divine love had always been available to me, inside of me, and all around me from the Source (Universe). I am supported and have always been gently nudged along the way with no judgment – just kindness and patience.

Now I know the truth, from deep within me, that by totally accepting and loving myself, I am able to support and empower myself and co-create a life I dream of with the power greater than me. This is the kind of self-empowerment that nothing and no one could ever take away from me. I just want to share this love and wisdom with others, so they too can start to see how to move on from their own painful past with Love.

If there is only one thing for you to take away from my story, let it be this: Your past does not define you. You are mightier than you believed about yourself. In fact, your force is so strong that you may have accidentally attracted toxic people out of fear, tolerated your own suffering, or allowed others to disrespect you longer than you need to. That is exactly why you are powerful enough to change everything you don't like in your life. You have the power to choose differently and to start taking your power back. You are not the victim as you once portrayed yourself to be. You are in fact a powerful manifestor who needs to be mindful about what you're creating in your life. And whatever you decide to create in your story, do it with love.

About the Author

Mina Love is a Self-Worth Coach for Moms, an artist, intuitive healer, and an advocate for child (emotional) safety. With her background in art and photography and her intuitive healing ability, Mina uses intentional creative activities to ground the teachings in personal development (mind) and traditional spiritual healing (soul) to heal her own wounded heart effectively after the deep betrayal and suicide of her late spouse and to create an unconditionally loving home for her children.

Mina's Creative Healing Magic Method is a set of strategical tools created to help make the healing and self-love journey enjoyable and practical for busy Moms who desire to rise above a toxic love in the past and own their true power.

Mina specializes in creating ways to help Moms optimize what they do to recharge themselves through her creative healing practices, so they can finally have the energy to connect with their children and create a safe and happy home for them. Mina hopes to prevent children from repeating the toxic relationship cycle of their family by empowering Moms.

Mina is currently loving her life with her two amazing children in Hawai'i. You can find out more about her at: https://www.creativehealingmagic.com/ or through her Instagram @thealohacoach.

SAM YOUNGZ

What and Who do You Keep Saying "Yes" to?

I was unsure of how to start this chapter or what elements of my toxic relationships to share with the world in 2022. I feel like my whole life has been full of toxicity in many different shapes and sizes! As I thought about what to write, my mind was a whirl of memories. I could feel the frustration rising within me as the page remained blank. I suppose this is what authors refer to as "writer's block." I trusted that the energy of the full moon would open up the flow of words, and as if by magic, a few days before the full Strawberry Supermoon, this popped into my mind: *"It*

starts with you. " Before I start to share my story, we need to travel back through time and space.

Millions of years ago scientists believe our universe was created with a big bang and the cosmic web of stars was born. The cosmic web contains dark matter and quantum energy fields and guess what! So do you. Our galaxy has been evolving and expanding when the right circumstances were present over millennia with the laws of nature. The birth of a new human life, all life, holds the echo of that original big bang and enters Earth with millions of years of stardust, nature, and your family ancestry. We are therefore connected and surrounded by quantum fields that are entangled by the past and the present, a universal DNA.

I now know my own birth holds multiple elements of webs and fields I needed to unravel. It took me four decades before I was willing and ready to put my own oxygen mask on and become an astronaut to explore the unknown space frontiers of my heart and soul stars. I was heading deep into the dark matter.

My conscious memory cannot recall my birth. We don't start consciously remembering life experiences until around the age of three. My first conscious memory is a vivid one and it isn't one that fills me with love. My subconscious and energetic bodies also remembered everything and had held onto my big bang entrance into this world for the huge trauma it was. My birth was kind of a taboo subject. No one spoke about it, and I now realise Mum had locked the trauma away somewhere deep inside her. She didn't like to talk about it – or anything else emotional, for that matter.

I was born at home which I believe was a planned decision. Something went very wrong during labour. Mum said, "All she can remember was lots of black stuff, the look of horror on the midwife's face, and my baby being whisked off with sirens. I didn't know if you were dead or alive." My medical records show that I was born with zero signs of life, and it took fifteen minutes to resuscitate me out of the zero scores. I was born dead and in total darkness. In the past, I have wished many times that it had stayed that way. At a foundational level, the theme and tone of my future relationships were set, and unconscious core belief seeds were planted.

I will be abandoned and remain all alone. I wasn't good enough. I'm unworthy. I don't belong. I'm insignificant and invisible. I'm not wanted. I'm going to die. Something awful is going to happen each time I try to start a new life cycle. Everything I know will be ripped away from me. These unconscious beliefs contributed to my reality. I had been born with very wrong ideas about what life could really offer me.

This chapter won't be sharing details about Mum for numerous reasons. When the time is right, the book she told me to write about my life will be born. There is probably enough content for a series of books! Our relationship with our Mum is the first relationship in every lifetime. We are learning from them inside the womb and every moment after we are born.

I have always had a desire to help others, and I knew I was here for a bigger purpose. I had this deep knowing inside, but it was locked away. I didn't know how to access what my life purpose was. I didn't have a clue who I truly was either. Here is what I did know though: there was more to this life than what I could see with my physical eyes.

I also knew I wanted to be of service in the holistic and spiritual field since my teenage years. I loved visiting mind-body-spirit fairs and wished I was there with my own stand. After I left my family home at sixteen, I was taken to my first spiritualist church by a friend's Mum. While writing this chapter, my friend's Mum, Barbara, died after a short illness with cancer. Thank you to your family for your kindness during such a dark period in my life, for introducing me to understanding more about the afterlife, and for reminding me that you can have colour in this life and the next. It isn't all darkness.

After I escaped my toxic home environment, I needed to find a way to earn money. I was 16, just sat my GCSE's and was meant to be going on to sixth form to study A Levels. I had to abort that plan. I needed to get a job to support myself. This is how I fell into a career in finance. I prefer numbers to words. Maths was my favourite subject at school. It made some sense that I eventually ended up as a qualified financial accountant in my 30s.

The financial sector is stressful. Bosses expect you to work overtime and to be able to wave magic wands to make budgets balance and profit margins grow. Working in a male dominated space can become quite toxic as a female. I witnessed male colleagues' careers be funded by our employers and become promoted time and time again over suitable females, including myself. I spent over ten years of part-time, self-financed home study to become a qualified accountant.

In my own experience, females in the finance world received inappropriate comments on what they were wearing, challenged about their figures in more ways than one, in the accuracy of accounts filed and how their physical body looked. I always felt like I wasn't good enough and had to prove myself by working harder than my male colleagues to get a fraction of the respect and pay they did. Once qualified I was well paid, still not as high as males mind. It would be hard to give up a steady five-figure salary that I had grown accustomed to. This toxic career in finance funded a lifestyle that I enjoyed - full of travel and adventure without an ounce of worry about my own personal finances.

Why did I spend so much money and time on a career that I ended up hating? I was trying to live up to the ideals and expectations of my dad. For him, money meant status, success, and love. He believed that you could buy love by bribing other people to do what you want and using your money to control them with gifts. This stems from his own traumatic childhood and resulted in me being an over-giver in all areas of my life. My Dad's toxic money and love mindset contributed to my lack of understanding about unconditional love and to my own toxic mindset about money. Going back to those birth core beliefs I mentioned earlier. I wanted to prove that I was good enough to be part of my family as a successful high-flying accountant.

But I wasn't living in a state of happiness. Along with working hard proving myself as good as my male colleagues. I was at the same time pinned down by such a heavy darkness since birth. Those pesky core beliefs were steering me here, there, and everywhere without my conscious agreement. How dare they!

I have repeatedly experienced all of the following since a young age, and I didn't know how to deal with them.

- Fatigue
- Burnout
- Frustration
- Stress
- Sadness
- Anxiety
- Physical pain
- Inability to say "No"
- Stuck in a rut
- Feeling invisible and not heard
- Unable to make decisions
- Can't seem to reach happiness
- Questioning: Who Am I? Why Am I Here?
- Fed up with being the 'strong one' and coming last

Can you relate?

I felt disconnected, unconfident, confused, and stuck in a rut deeper than the Grand Canyon. I trusted no one and felt like no one liked me. I felt responsible for everyone else and operated 24/7 in rescue mode. This weight of responsibility led me to put others first and to feel like a victim of life.

How did I deal with this big ball of internal messiness that was a bubbling pressure cooker waiting to explode? I built up huge concrete walls around my heart, fiercely independent, kept everyone at arm's length and became a professional binge drinker. I dabbled in recreational Class B drugs too, but the only thing that stopped me from becoming addicted to class A drugs was the fact that my brother became an addict and died from an overdose – the heartbreaking impact of our dysfunctional family on us both.

Did his death stop me from being in self-destruct mode? Nope. I headed further down that destructive path and tried to escape the pain of his death by completely upping sticks. I waved goodbye to the UK, my few close friends, the family member I was still in touch with, and moved to live and work abroad in Bermuda as a Hedge Fund Accountant. Believe me when I tell you that an expat lifestyle combined with self-destructive tendencies is not a good mix. In my opinion, most expats are running away from something they are not yet ready to face.

The job was so stressful with long hours, so my solution was to party even harder. Drinking champagne out of bottles on a dancefloor around 2 am wasn't unusual for me. I got the nickname Champs! Turning up to work still under the influence of alcohol and on a couple of hours of sleep became the norm. I had to be the last person standing at the end of the night. I also wasn't eating regularly or healthily.

When I registered with a British GP in Bermuda, she gave me a warning: "If you have a problem with alcohol, this island will only make it worse." I told a big, fat lie to her (and myself) when I replied, "That isn't relevant to me. I don't have a problem." Who the hell was I trying to kid? My whole immediate family had big issues with alcohol in an attempt to avoid facing their own internal pressure cookers of pain. Humans are wired to seek pleasure and avoid discomfort and pain. Your method of avoiding pain may be different from mine. You might comfort eat, buy things you don't really need or can't afford, gamble, exercise excessively, put work life before your personal life or any other mode of pleasure-seeking. I still wasn't ready to face my emotional pain and continued down that rollercoaster path of self-destruction and sabotage.

Until my physical body could no longer support this way of toxic living, I had ignored the warning signs for years. In Bermuda, I started to develop allergies, asthma, skin issues, and hormonal issues. Fatigue has always been lurking, but I've always managed to push through. My body screamed, "If you are not going to listen, I am going to put you out of action until you do!"

At the age of 37, the same age my brother was when he died, my body went bang. I had ignored a strange migraine for 24 hours and went out to celebrate St Patrick's Day, with champagne, of course! The next morning, I woke up feeling ill but in a way I had never felt before. I went to stand up and immediately fell over. The whole room was moving around me. This was the beginning of months in bed trying to find out what was wrong. Every time I tried to return to work, I would be violently ill again and stuck in bed trying to regain some energy. Fortunately, living in Bermuda, I had access to quality private health care.

After months of intensive tests, I was diagnosed with Myalgic Encephalomyelitis/Chronic Fatigue Syndrome (ME/CFS) and told to take at least a year off from work to try to recover. I had to reduce the stress levels in my body, because it had become toxic to itself, both inside and out.

The year was 2010, and I had to leave the island of Bermuda. My work visa was invalid as I was unable to work. I hadn't planned on returning to the UK. Where was I going to go back to and how was I going to survive not being able to work? Leaving in this ill state was a journey into hell that in turn opened up the gateway to deep personal emotional healing and discovery.

Twelve years later, I still feel some of the effects of the way I treated my body for those 30+ years before 2010. I've also discovered that I have genetic conditions. Discovering I was born with EDS (Ehlers Danlos Syndrome) was a lightbulb moment. It made sense of the weird health issues that I had experienced since childhood that had been dismissed as nothing and growing pains. It turns out that I was not just "attention seeking." EDS is a connective tissue disorder that impacts every body system function and can predispose some to chronic fatigue and pain. It wasn't all in my head why my body felt worn out and hurt as a child.

I don't believe I would have quit the finance sector, the alcohol, the cigarettes, or the unhealthy lifestyle that I had been living if my body had not had that big bang in 2010. I would not have discovered my life purpose or gone on a roller coaster of a healing journey either. Stopping me in my tracks for a good couple of years was exactly what I needed to happen, but I don't want others to reach this point before starting their own recovery and discovery journey.

I am not a religious person per se, but I do believe in the afterlife, galactic star beings, and spiritual guides because I have experience with all of them. If anything, I would say I am more drawn to the spiritual practices of Eastern cultures. I am fascinated by ancient civilizations and their traditions which tend to be based on what was happening in the sky, stars, and on Earth.

My birthday is known as Epiphany in the Christian calendar – not something I've taken any notice of until recent years. It dawned on me that Epiphany was linked to the stars and comes from the Greek word for manifestation. On Epiphany, the three Wise Men had followed a bright star in the night sky to seek higher truths, the meaning of life, and this journey led them to new life. Their journey was not without its obstacles, people who were seeking to take advantage of them for their own means, and others who fully supported their pathway to the truth. I think many of us can relate to these different types of people.

To create a life that was a joy to live, no longer caught up in the webs of the past, I needed to follow my own heart and soul stars. To do that successfully, I needed to heal by accepting the truth of my own existence, warts, and all. There were many layers to unravel and dots to connect.

Another one of these layers and dots was being told by a psychologist I had been living with PTSD since childhood. I was diagnosed in 2018 with emotional trauma past and present after trying to find answers to why my mental health had gone into crisis. The PTSD diagnosis took a while to get my head around, I remember staring at the psychologist in total disbelief and shock. I have experienced phases of anxiety and depression before, but I held the belief that PTSD was only experienced by those that had witnessed or experienced horrific events such as service and emergency personnel.

I was not a paranoid, strange, unlikeable child who sought attention as I had been told by an adult (not Mum). I was a scared, traumatised human in survival mode where the world had made no sense for so long and not knowing how to deal with my chain of adverse life experiences since birth.

As more emotional healing dots have been pieced together, I've silenced the voices that once told me, "Keep quiet! Don't say anything! Just keep the peace. Don't rock the boat!" Now, I have learned to find my own voice again, to put myself first, and to un-apologetically reveal who I am.

I didn't have a grand plan for my healing journey. I've been led by life events, intuition, and nudges from the universe which I haven't fully listened to for many years. I was given a clear message at the age of 24 after my Nan died following a decade of living with dementia. I had been trying to figure out the meaning of life and find a source of comfort for my grief. I visited a local Buddhist centre. It felt so calm and peaceful there. I wandered around and started to read some information boards. As I read the words "break the cycle," I felt like I had been struck by a lightning bolt.

In that instant, I knew that I needed to "break the cycle" for myself and my whole family. I was the one that had to break the toxic cycles and repeating patterns, it didn't start to happen until nearly two decades later. I was literally repeating history with the abusive relationships I entered into during my early adult years. One of these nearly cost me my life after trying to end the relationship and break free of its trauma bond. My partner at that time was adamant he was not letting me go, and no one else was going to have me either.

This life journey has been full of both internal and external conflicts. For decades, I had no personal boundaries. When I started saying "no," I was not met with open arms by those who could no longer manipulate and gaslight me. Putting personal boundaries in place has caused a loss of relationships, some by choice, some not. Don't get me wrong, while losing relationships was painful at the time, the outcome is now having those in my life who support me.

You will have your own starting point, something that triggers you to finally say, "Enough is enough! I can't keep living like this. Something has got to change." Mine was a severe physical illness.

I'd love to share a couple of tips to support you as you move from putting yourself last to putting yourself first. I personally use these tips regularly, and they have helped build my resilience to cope with life better.

Tip #1: Practice Gratitude.

Your brain has a negativity bias and the vast majority of your day, tens of thousands of thoughts are unknown as they happen automatically in your subconscious mind. Gratitude helps us to shift this negative bias and open up to appreciate what we have in life, even during the most challenging of times. This is not dismissing anything that you are struggling with but helping you cope with it better.

Start a daily gratitude practice of writing down three new things that you are grateful for. These don't need to be big things. For example, "I am grateful for seeing a rainbow, having a bed to sleep on, and sunny mornings." Choose a time of day that suits you best so that you can easily form this new habit. Most people find that early morning or late evening are the best times. You don't need a fancy gratitude journal. A simple notebook will do to get started.

There are many benefits of practising gratitude:[4]

- Rewire your brain
- Improve sleep
- Improve relationships
- Help people heal and grow, even PTSD victims
- Help people recover from/with mental physical and emotional pain
- Increase resilience in adults and young people
- Heal for our bodies
- Release oxytocin
- Move you from a mindset of lack to abundance
- Improve mental and physical health
- Support human flourishing

Tip #2: Connect with Nature.

In essence, you are nature. We all come from stardust. When we have toxic influences in life, a way to reduce their impact is to work with the cycles and rhythms of nature. Nature was here long before humans were, and it has evolved, adapted and flourished. Working in harmony with the seasons, moon cycles, and daily cycles will help to balance your energy fields and connect you to a healing energy field instead of toxic ones. Switching

---

[4] "Greater Good Science Center." *Greater Good Science Center*, https://ggsc.berkeley.edu/.

to certified natural medicines, skincare, personal care, and wellbeing products also helps reduce the stress on your organs. In the modern world, we are engulfed by so much pollution and technology that disrupts our natural flow of life.

If you aren't yet ready to face breaking the cycles of your toxic ties, a daily connection with nature will be a supportive friend for you. Take time in green spaces to smell flowers, sit against trees, gaze at stars, stand barefoot on grass/sand, allow the wind to blow through your hair and listen to its whispers. As your nature connection grows, you can start to notice how you feel during the different phases of the day, moon and seasons. You can learn from nature that balance is required to flourish. There are times to receive and go inwards, and there are times to shine brightly and give outwards.

The title of this chapter is *What and Who do you keep saying "Yes" to?* Are you able to say "yes" to yourself and "no" to others? I'd like you to honestly answer these questions. There is no judgement or criticism in doing so. Just a moment of reflection and opportunity. I had not said "yes" to myself in a healthy way for 37 years. Here are the three things I wished someone had told me from a young age:

1. I am not responsible for anyone else's happiness.
2. I will not make people like me more by being available 24/7.

3. Keep saying *"Yes"* to the needs of others does not make me a better person.

Healing your heart by processing and releasing emotions that you have held onto is the energetic gateway to opening up your connection to your higher purpose and living a joyful life. Just like the stars that have guided humankind since ancient times, you have internal stars that can guide you safely: your heart and soul. It's time to activate your heart and soul potential so you can sparkle inside and out!

To start your star healing journey, I have created a chakra energy grid of colour and sacred geometry for this chapter and book. Please say the word 'Starlight' three times to activate this for yourself. Get in touch with me if you would like a digital download of the grid.

If you are an empathic, spiritual woman who is here to help serve others, but you are confused about your purpose and disconnected from the answers you are seeking. Life has left you feeling worn out, invisible, frustrated, and stressed. You spend all your time giving to everyone else and can't shake off what is holding you back. This was me until a few years ago, and I don't want you to spend years trying to break free of destructive patterns like I did.

If you desire to say "yes" to yourself and feel a connection to my words, you may feel called to gently travel into your dark matter with my emotional energy therapies. We can work together to empower you to restore a renewed resilience, vitality, and healthy pleasure in life. You will understand how you can stop exhausting your own energy reserves, listen to your own inner stars, and recognize the needs of your whole holistic self with a sense of freedom. You will be able to trust your initiative and intuition to make the changes needed to create a vibrant future. I am able to support you to do this as I have created it for myself.

It all starts with *you* – just like this chapter and my healing all started with me. My purpose is to share my story, wisdom, and healing so that you can do the same to live your purpose.

PS - You won't become a selfish cow by putting your needs first when you are doing so from a place of kindness, compassion, and awareness.

About the Author

Sam Youngz empowers empathic women to move from feeling worn out and frustrated of being known as the 'strong one' to the freedom of understanding themselves better with improved energy and relationships so that they can put themselves first guilt-free.

Forming healthy boundaries physically and emotionally *is* possible. Sam gently guides you on a journey of multi-dimensional exploration that allows you to access your own inner wisdom and improve your spiritual connection so that you can heal your heart at a deeper level.

As a Psychic Energy Healer and Holistic Wellness Advisor offering therapeutic services and products under her full name RubySamYoungZ. Sam works with powerful energy modalities, emotions, spirit, and nature to release you from repeating life patterns keeping you stuck in a loop of people-pleasing to freedom to be who you truly are at your soul level.

Sam's own childhood and life experiences give her a special interest in supporting women who have been impacted by domestic violence, dysfunctional families, addictions, maternal relationships, and chronic invisible illnesses.

Parts of Sam's life story have been featured on the BBC, Heart Radio, and in media articles for Spirit and Destiny, The Telegraph, The Mail, and The Sun. She was also featured on the most downloaded podcast episode on Soulful Valley titled Unravelling Trauma.

Sam lives in Shropshire, UK with her fluffy rescue dog and can be found regularly admiring the wonders of the sky, universe, and mother earth. She particularly loves flowers, crystals, Weleda, stars, and laughing.

You can connect with Sam online at: https://linktr.ee/RubySamYoungZ

Please request the free digital download mentioned in the chapter via email at: rubysamyoungz@gmail.com She would love to hear your thoughts about this courageous, inspiring book.

SARAH BRIGID BROWN

The Shifting of Consciousness:
From Victim and Rescuer to
Coach and Creator

My heart is very sensitive and easily touched. One of the things I find unbearable is to hear and see other people's painful feelings and suffering because I can feel all of this, too.

I used to be so in tune with their feelings that there was no room for my own. I was unaware of the damage I was doing to myself, my body, and my soul by choosing to ignore the signals I was getting, brushing them off as if it didn't matter, and believing they were dangerous. As a child, I learnt that feelings can be both used as a weapon and seemingly non-existent. As far as I could sense, there was no room for my emotivity, vulnerability or authenticity.

So, I disconnected from it all – big time. I disguised my fear by putting myself in dangerous situations, as if to prove that I was fearless. I silenced my need for unconditional love by betraying my soul. I rejected my intuition by listening to other people who I thought knew better than me or who were manipulating me without me even realising.

I reached a point where I had completely denied who I was. A point where I was convinced that everyone would leave me and that I wouldn't be loved if I was myself.

At the time, I had no idea that I didn't love myself and that I was, in fact, the person who had left, who had abandoned me. It took me many, many years to come back to my true, authentic self, and during some of those years, I needed help from doctors and medicine. Little by little, I became a medicine woman for myself, finding strength within, reconnecting to the beauty of Nature, and learning to heal through forgiveness, journalling, and energy work.

What I share here is probably also true for you because we ARE our own medicine – what we feed ourselves can either nurture us or poison us. Healthy relationships with ourselves and those who we choose to surround ourselves with nurture us; toxic relationships, on the other hand, poison us very subtly, in ways that we may find hard to imagine and understand.

You see, this is the insidious thing about this kind of relationship – most of the time, we don't even know that we are in one until it's too late, and we feel so trapped and entangled that we don't know what to do, feeling like prey in a spider's web. Much like an innocent, winged insect, despite our best efforts to get ourselves out and to set ourselves free, we can end up getting even more caught up in the toxicity. We remain trapped until something happens to really open our eyes to all the manipulation, emotional blackmail, abuse, and downright lies. Some people call them "wake-up calls;" I call these moments the "shifting of consciousness."

The shift first started to really happen for me back in 2008 when I began seeing a psycho-energetic therapist following a life-changing health problem. I had been diagnosed with a massive, slipped disc at the base of my spine and refused to undergo surgery to remove it. I needed to heal, and thanks to my doctor and his support, I agreed to investigate alternative ways that aligned better with my convictions.

This was the first time I had had therapy, so I turned up at the first session not knowing what to expect from it. My therapist soon brought up the subject of my close family and my family tree, and together, we began to unravel the energetic knots that I was caught up in.

One of the first emotions to come up for me was self-judgement. How could I have let myself be manipulated like that? How could I have let people who I loved and who were supposed to love me take advantage of my sensitivity and empathy? How could I have allowed them to make me feel like I was responsible for their happiness and self-esteem?

I had never heard of the words "narcissist" or "toxic guilt" before 2008. What I was on the verge of discovering would forever change my life and my relationships, and eventually lead me to become the coach, teacher, and healer that I am today.

But before I share this part of my story, I want to talk to you about the child I once was. My coming into the world wasn't planned, but I didn't know this until I was in my mid-teens. By the time I found out, I had already taken on so much responsibility that wasn't mine and was really struggling to fit in. No matter what I did, it just didn't seem to make much of a difference because the feeling of being rejected – or, at least, not being accepted for who I really was – had become a part of my daily life.

I was rejected for being 'too emotional' or 'so serious.' I was rejected because I didn't want to do things like everyone else. I now obviously realise that being sensitive, empathetic, and different are superpowers, but back then, nothing was further from the truth.

I had learnt to hide what I was feeling for fear of being judged or criticised. I didn't know that this would lead me to totally numb myself out and show up as a cold, distant, and arrogant person. Those who have met me in recent years find it hard to believe when I tell them how things used to be. I had turned into someone

I didn't recognise, someone I didn't like, and someone who was slowly sinking with no one to throw her a lifeline.

Walking on eggshells became the norm. I constantly felt as if I was to blame for other people's problems. Oh, the guilt trips I went on, some of my own making but most of them, as an unwilling passenger. These trips took me so far away from myself, from my essence, and made me question my self-worth and my ability to be unconditionally loved.

I let so many people take advantage of my insecurities, and I betrayed myself so many times. The web had been woven, and it would take me nearly forty years to start unravelling it. Little did I know that when my therapist and I started to pull on the threads, it would lead to such self-discovery, release, and empowerment.

Quite early on in my therapy, I was introduced to the Karpman Drama Triangle. You may be familiar with this, but I wasn't. Let me briefly explain what it is. The Karpman Drama Triangle is a tool used to map out destructive interaction between two people who are emotionally intertwined. Karpman defined three roles in such relationships – the Victim, the Persecutor, and the Rescuer. To keep things simple, we can say that the Victim will adopt a "Poor me!" attitude, the Persecutor will say or imply "It's all your fault!" and the Rescuer's response will be "Let me help you!"

Persecutors can be controlling, judgmental and aggressive. They blame and make others feel guilty as a means of protecting themselves and put others down so that they can feel okay in themselves. Critical parents who feel the need to always be right, tend to blame their children and make them feel guilty, and in doing so, become Persecutors. Children of parents like this will automatically become Victims, and in turn, either become Persecutors or Rescuers when they are tired of being Victims.

Victims feel trapped and helpless, complain that their needs are unmet, deny their dreams and discount their own ability to find a solution to the situation they find themselves in. They place their happiness in other people's hands, while Rescuers take responsibility for what isn't theirs to carry.

Without realising it, I took on the role of Rescuer at an early age. I loved and still love helping people, but now my motivations have changed. In the past, I was seeking approval, acceptance, and love from others. Today, I am seeking acceptance, love, and reliance on self.

On the outside, and especially from the Victim's point of view, being a Rescuer is fantastic! We sweep in to save the world with the skills that we have subconsciously picked up over the years: reading people's energy, rushing to their side as soon as they need help, and doing our utmost to make them happy.

Except here's the thing – being a Rescuer leads to us feeling overworked, exhausted, stuck, and resentful, because we make so many sacrifices just to help those in need. On the rare occasions we don't step up to help, guilt immediately creeps in because we aren't fulfilling the role we have chosen. And so, it continues, until we are forced or decide to step out of the triangle.

ENTANGLED NO MORE

"How people treat you is their karma; how you react is yours."
Wayne Dyer

Have you ever heard someone say that karma is good or bad? I am sure you have. I much prefer Wayne Dyer's description, as it takes us away from the status of Victim and leads us towards personal empowerment. Taking responsibility for ourselves, our emotions, and our reactions to the way others treat us is an essential part of the disentanglement process. Becoming disentangled can be really difficult, especially when the other person doesn't want to loosen their grip.

In my experience, as you start to establish boundaries, the Persecutors will try, by all possible means, to reinforce their control over you and push you over the edge. This has happened to me several times. I have been called undeserving (*"You don't deserve your husband, your children, etc."*), unlovable (*"look at you, I hate you!"* coming from a place of jealousy, or *"it's no wonder you don't have any friends"* when I was trying to build up new friendships), and ungrateful or selfish (*"after all I've done for you"*, or *"If you loved me, you would..."*).

These are just a few examples of the emotional abuse I suffered for a large part of my life, all the while thinking this was normal behaviour until one particular incident that led to the spreading of lies about me. We were housing a family member and it wasn't always easy to share our living space. Things came to a head one evening and after a heated argument, this person decided to leave. At the time, I didn't know that she had not only contacted one of my close friends to ask if she could go there, but she had also started telling friends and family that I had kicked her out. I was lucky enough to have my friend looking out for me, and she told me what was going on behind my back. I was absolutely devastated. It felt like I had been slapped in the face and the feelings of betrayal and rejection resurfaced. I wondered about the action I needed to take to put things right. That was enough for me to start what I can now call a disengagement from extremely toxic behaviour. It wasn't easy at the start; there were times when I felt like I had to defend myself for something I hadn't done, like I was part of a smear campaign.

As Jill Blakeway said, *"When a toxic person can no longer control you, they will try to control how others see you. The misinformation will feel unfair, but stay above it, trusting that other people will eventually see the truth, just like you did."*

This resonates so much with me because I felt wrongly accused, judged, and found guilty without a fair trial. Most people involved in this incident believed what the other person was saying, until they were also on the receiving end of such toxicity. There were times that I struggled to rise above it, yet with hindsight, this was helping me to build up my inner strength.

When I began to break free from toxic relationships, I realised that I was totally disconnected from my intuition and my inner knowing. Being on the receiving end of mind games had led me to dismiss these flashes of inspiration and to wonder if there was

272

something fundamentally wrong with me. Once I started to understand everything that had been going on for all these years, and the way I had been led to believe that my reactions to this behaviour were toxic, rather than the behaviour itself, that is when I began to set myself free.

"The day I started to heal my past was the day I set myself free."
Sarah Brigid Brown

I'm not one for regrets, but when I look back at some of the most important decisions in my life (selling a house, buying a house, and choosing a childminder for my children, for example), I can see the way I let this self-doubt and mistrust of myself seep in. At the time, I didn't have the courage to stand up for what I was feeling inside, and so I let others influence my decisions.

I agreed to go through with the sale of our house, despite sensing that it would fall through. Unfortunately, it did, because one of the buyers had a life-threatening disease unbeknown to us and couldn't get a mortgage. This put my young family in an extremely uncomfortable and stressful financial situation.

I reluctantly agreed to buy a house, even though I felt very unsettled when we went to visit it. Several unbelievable things happened to make us think twice but we bought it anyway. We missed our flight home after a family wedding in Paris, through no fault of our own, and had to wait hours to rent a car to get us back to Toulouse before the next morning, so that our eldest son could sit his exams. The bank lost our mortgage application two months into the buying process, and we had to start from scratch again. Our three children and my parents-in-law narrowly escaped a fatal accident on the motorway on their way back from holiday. These are just a few events that made me start questioning the purchase of this particular house. When my husband and I ended up on the verge of divorce years later, we discovered that it was also the home of two spirits who hadn't transitioned to the higher realms. In hindsight, that was the reason why I had felt unsettled.

On two separate occasions, I left two of my children with very domineering women when I went back to work after maternity leave, despite feeling sick inside and knowing that I wasn't doing the right thing. I did this because we had originally said that we were interested in hiring them and I felt like I couldn't go back on my word. My children weren't looked after by these women for long but one of them suffered physically and psychologically for years after.

Now I look back, I understand how I came to mistrust other women, never felt safe in their company, and thought I had to compete with them. There were fortunately the odd friends who really got me and who have been there for me despite the geographical distance between us, especially a loving, genuine woman called Wendy. She has been by my side through everything – happy and sad, challenging and exciting. She has shown me that a healthy friendship is full of support, unconditional acceptance and understanding of another person.

Thanks to the unwavering love and encouragement of these friends and some family members, I have been able to heal my own wounds, feel accepted and respected, and overcome the challenges I used to face in certain relationships. I really started to love and accept myself and to recognise my inner power in 2018, by reconnecting to the spirit of Brigid, the Celtic goddess, the day after I finished a spiritual coaching retreat. I was drawn to a deck of oracle cards in a small apothecary in San Francisco and to Brigid. Her message was: *"Don't back down; stand up for what you believe is right."* This has since become a motto for me, especially when I'm unsure about speaking up about my needs and my deepest truth. Yet the more I speak my truth, the clearer my intentions become, the lighter my energy feels, and the more aligned, connected, and purposeful I am.

I want to leave you with a Medicine Woman's Prayer, as it really sums up the way I coach, teach, and guide people.

"I will not rescue you, for you are not powerless.
I will not fix you, for you are not broken.
I will not heal you, for I see you in your wholeness.
I will walk with you through the darkness,
as you remember your light."

If you are ready to reconnect to your inner wisdom, transcend your past, and break free of your chains, I would be honoured to walk beside you.

About the Author

Sarah Brigid Brown is a speaker, coach, teacher, author, and nurturer creating a safe and empathetic space for sensitive, emotional people who feel like outsiders, to show them the way to get to the root of what's stopping them from moving forwards. She does this by accompanying them on a journey to shift their past narrative, overcome their pain, and awaken to their truth. This leads them to put an end to the toxic relationships they have with themselves and their mothers, get clear on what they really desire, and be brave enough to connect to their own wisdom, inner strength, and power to finally become leaders of their best lives, rise up, and be themselves!

Sarah knows exactly what it is like to do this, as she went from being a people pleaser, always wanting to control everything, afraid to speak up, and totally disconnected from who she *really* was, to a passionate coach, teacher, and guide, in love with life, following her calling to help as many people as possible, embracing all her imperfections, and believing in a future where love and community reign.

Sarah's approach is very holistic, as she is trained in neurolinguistic, emotional, and energy healing techniques. She loves letting her intuition guide her towards the modalities that would best serve each individual person and holding space for people to learn to rely on their own power and resources.

She is one of the co-authors of Evolving on Purpose, an Amazon international best-selling book published by Soulful Valley and currently available as a paperback and eBook from Amazon, and soon available as an audiobook. She is also the creator and producer of guided meditations, visualisations, and EFT (tapping) sequences available on her YouTube channel.

She currently lives in the south of France with her husband, two cats and close to her three adult children.

To connect with Sarah, visit her website: https://www.so-free.life/en/home Also, please enjoy a free EFT sequence for empaths here: https://www.youtube.com/watch?v=kwzDDU3ZJS4

SOLVEIG BERG

My Chameleon Self and I

S he is such a sweetie and so calm."
We were visiting one of my mom's friends for coffee and cake. I was approximately five years old and playing on the floor beside the coffee table.

"Yes, she is – finally. She was such a difficult baby – crying through the nights and a lot of illnesses and problems with her. But now she's really making up for it," my mom answered.

I had heard this conversation before – not exactly the same words but the same content. I had to make up for it, and I not only had to make up for it, I *wanted* to make up for it. I mean, who voluntarily wants to be a pain in the a...? We all want to be loved; we want to be accepted; we want to be good human beings. We want to be part of our tribe.

Around the time that my mom had this conversation with her friend, my chameleon-self was born – the part of me that developed an automatism of fitting in, of camouflaging into the expectation of others, loved ones or authorities. For the longest part of my life, I was perfect Solveig – "sooo nice, sooo calm, sooo good." I loved taking this reward.

In hindsight, I am realizing that no one said to me directly: "Be this way or be that way." My unconscious adaptation was always derived from other people's worldviews or experiences.

Let's take Sister Thecla in elementary school. She was a nun from our city's monastery representing a very fundamental Catholic belief system which she permanently integrated into our school day – not only when religion was on the schedule, but throughout all classes. She told us horror stories about Hell and which horrible people would end up there. It goes without saying that I was not one of those horrible people. And if I ever went into one of those hell traps (and believe me, there were many as the Ten Commandments are not easily fulfilled by a little girl), I rushed into church to confess.

Today, it makes me laugh and cry at the same time, because what I felt so terrifyingly bad about were sins like eating too much chocolate, fighting with my siblings, or scrolling through the lingerie section of a big warehouse catalogue.

Once a week, I even went to church service at 7 am before school started. I hated it, but being a good girl seemed safe, especially also because of my dad who never went to church. Not being in church on a Sunday, according to Sister Thecla, meant the safest way to Hell. Somebody had to compensate for my dad. As a kind of reward, I got to play the role of the Holy Francis in our school play at the end of the term. I looked like Holy Mary in a light blue headscarf doing the praying hands throughout the whole play. I enjoyed the attention given to me by Sister Thecla.

I was so perfect in adapting and fitting in that I never got a bad word from any teacher. Solveig was a nice and uncomplicated girl, calm and reliable, very mature for her age, and she always passed dictates without any spelling error.

In high school, things changed a bit. There was one side of me still being a perfect chameleon, but another side getting more and more visible: Solveig the Rebel. I do not mean the usual teenage rebellion that we all have to go through to find our identity. There was a deep knowing that school was not right, that this society was not right.

I was naturally a good student even though I was rather lazy and unmotivated. My good grades and my reputation as a reliable student gave me space to use for my own agenda. My classmates elected me to class representative nearly every term. I happily held this office not because of my sense of responsibility for the class or to initiate new projects. It gave me time away from classes, space to just sit and dream in representatives' meetings and take myself out of the usual buzz and noise of school.

As soon as I was legally allowed to sign my own absence excuse notes, I had an absence rate of 60% - that means three days a week I stayed away from school. How was that possible? I had my room downstairs at the basement level but with my own terrace door out into the garden. Every other morning, I went out of the main door, saying good-bye to my parents pretending to go to school but instead went just around the house, through my open terrace door back into my room and crawled back into my bed.

As my parents both were at their working places throughout mornings, it was only the cleaning lady noticing me staying at home. Why she never ever said one single word about that to my mom, I do not know until today. Still grateful for her keeping quiet!

I chose my absence days wisely, never missing tests and giving the teachers the opportunities to get their grades for me. I still had rather good grades, so there never was an open complaint from a teacher. This was when I realized that my chameleon-self also could serve me in staying under the radar, still avoiding conflict, sparing me to fully stand up for myself and my needs and letting me live out some of my other aspects.

My chameleon-self kept on dominating the biggest part of my life. In my first really long relationship, I was with a very self-confident and strong man who understood how to lead me in such a way that I was totally living his life – not mine. I got my sailing licenses when he suggested (never ever used them again since our breakup). I studied at the university where he was already attending. After university, he got me a PhD position at the institute he was already working in. He even got me out of bed earlier as I wanted to go every weekend to his favourite spots (mostly to his parents' place). The weird thing was that he always asked me: "What would you like to do? Alternative A, which is so great and just imagine the fun and excitement... Or alternative B (voice going down, excitement gone)?" Well, guess what my chameleon-self chose?

My breakdown came in 2016, when I was already married with two kids and fell in love with another man. This is when I should have taken a clear decision, but I did not, and my chameleon-self consequently had to crash between two diametrically confronting realities. In the end, there was no man and only me with myself. Outwardly, my chameleon-self kept me functioning but inside I was a wreck, crying secretly in the lonely moments and getting deeper and deeper into depression.

When I finally got out of depression in 2018, I promised myself: NO compromising anymore. I had always been spiritually interested and active, but I was just now beginning what I would call "my serious awareness and wake-up journey." My chameleon-self did not disappear from one day to the other. Just recently, I became aware of rather subtle ways it still is active. Awareness is an ongoing process of what I call dis-identification from old beliefs and automatisms. For me personally, it is a long journey of getting aware of so-called chameleon-offers and refusing them.

What helped me getting aware of chameleon offers?

When I started out on my awareness journey in 2018, I only knew that I wanted to live my life instead of constantly having the feeling that my life was living me – turning me into a ping pong ball played around by outer circumstances. I wanted to take control and do whatever was needed to make my dreams come true instead of waiting and hoping without any tangible results.

I had a lot of ideas, and my first decision was to invest into a big coaching program to start my online business as a coach with a money loan from my mother. In this coaching, we had to get clear on objectives and goals in life – small ones, medium ones, and big ones. Soon, it became crystal clear that it was no longer possible to go for my own needs and goals and be a chameleon at the same time.

The biggest challenge was to not fall into chameleon-self in relation to my potential customers. I realized that it was not hard to draw boundaries towards collective beliefs and paradigms (like changing from a more male professional attitude of working hard to a more female attitude of receiving), but I surely wanted to please potential customers as I was afraid of ruining my business from the start. This led to problems in price-setting and having women literally pouring their energy out on me in our free conversations. It goes without saying that winning customers was really hard and barely successful.

By getting to know about the law of attraction and our ability as creators of our reality, things opened up and got more and more clear to me. I finally realized that by adapting to the expectation of others and making myself smaller, I also kept other people's creative space smaller. I realized that we all are in search of and in need of certain energetic food according to old automatisms. What I was doing by pleasing others and fitting smoothly in was actually counteracting all change. I was giving other people their old food over and over again not serving them at all. And I had been serving myself the least. It was a lose-lose situation.

I had to get clear on my own inner standards and boundaries. I had to learn to dare to say a simple "No" without legitimizing my answer by rational arguments. I learned that "no" is a whole sentence, and I learned to keep my mouth shut after saying "no."

I got clear on what it means for me to have integrity with myself, and I experienced the enormous power of following this integrity and keeping to my standards. I dared to speak my truth and also be the trigger for others in my environment. Many turned away and split ways with me, but new ones came. And I can definitely say that my whole environment changed for the good. I am surrounded by friends and customers that are on the same path and where there is an understanding without words. It turned into a win-win-situation.

Let's take prices as a concrete example: Whenever a woman and potential customer told me about her situation as a single mother having financially hard times and a difficult situation in her job, I was already inside of me going down with my price. I even felt bad about offering coaching at all. I had thoughts about being a good person only if I would offer my services for free.

But what would have been the result? I would have confirmed to that woman her self-image of being poor and unable to make her dreams possible. I would have taken myself down instead of inviting her up.

Potential customers have the choice to turn away or take the invitation and step up to their own next level. I remember so many occasions now where a new customer told me the story about how they manifested the money for my training not knowing how but trusting in their creator's power and willing to take the steps to lift themselves up to a higher level.

In my own coaching with my 1:1 mentor, I worked constantly on what she calls "boundaries." For me, this was mostly the confrontation with my chameleon-self. And confrontation is not only about throwing something out or fighting against it and winning. I have come to terms with my chameleon-self, and this is an ongoing process of constantly balancing out. Because in the end, the chameleon-self hints to a huge gift – the gift of empathy, connectedness to others and everything around us. It is the gift of clairsentience as you can feel the other's issues and stories behind what they are saying and how they are behaving.

For me, the challenge was to discern actual issues – here the story of a person about money being scarce and standing between them and my offer – and their creator's ability – being able to take a new choice and change despite these stories or issues. Thus, I was able to stick to my prices and offer them the opportunity to take a closer look at their beliefs about money and their money mindset. Being finally able to discern these two aspects made me become the valued and appreciated coach that I am today.

Did you recognize your own chameleon-self at some point in this text?

We all have this aspect in us, but we all can come to terms with our own chameleon and receive the huge gift and growth by elevating awareness and consciousness about our own inner automatisms.

The chameleon-self is born out of our fear of not being loved, not being accepted as we are, the fear of falling out of our tribe, our family, our peer group, or society. We strive to please everyone, to fit in as smoothly as possible. It is about an anticipatory obedience to take over roles and identities rather unconsciously offered by others. It is also about keeping energetic taboos as they are, not addressing them but rather serving and enforcing them even more by "playing the game."

Those roles and identities we unconsciously take over can be general as that of a mother, an entrepreneur, a lover, or a coach.

Every role and identity is connected to a bunch of expectations, beliefs and behavioural codes.

The media is constantly offering categories, roles, and identities. Right now, in this moment of writing, it is about people who vaccinate themselves or don't. A majority of people right now are desperately trying to stay out of the role of "conspiracy theorist" like this would be the worst label ever.

Whenever there is a sports championship, the media plays with identities by using headlines such as "We have won" or "We have lost." Once in German media, when Pope Benedict was elected, the headline even said "we are pope".

But those roles and identities can come disguised in even more subtle ways. I will give you two of my own examples which were big game changers when I recognized them as chameleon offers:

1. *"I have been with so many coaches now, no one could help me. But with you, I have the feeling that you are the one that can help me."* I have fallen a few times for these offered roles: the "rescue coach," the one and only. It goes without saying that the cooperation with these customers turned out to be a catastrophe. Today, whenever I hear this sentence, I decline this potential customer.

2. *"All my other ex-girlfriends always complained about me, but with you, I feel that you will never be like them."* Guess what? I would have liked to complain about a lot of things with this man, but never

dared as I was surely not as bad as his ex-girl-friends...

I dare you to do three things:

1. **Set standards.** What is it that you desire in life? What is it you REALLY want? Write it down. Commit yourself to it. This life happens only once, and time is a limited resource. What kind of parent would YOU like to be? What kind of entrepreneur? You can create your own rules, your own principles, and stick to them.

2. **Say "No."** It is one of the most liberating moments when you dare to say "No." I always remember myself being in terror and panic just knowing I should set my boundary and say "No." It often takes enormous courage and my way to navigate this is to just do it as quickly as possible to be over with it. The feeling afterwards is so rewarding as I can literally feel my space expanding and power growing from speaking my truth. This boundary-setting is easier from time to time as I never had the experience of being punished. It is rather the contrary: People respecting and acknowledging me for taking these steps and naming me as a role model. I even got the feedback from a customer not long ago: You are so clear about your offers – what it contains and what

it does not contain. There is no doubt about it, and this helps me extremely well.

3. **Polarize, trigger and break taboos.** I would not only say that you should dare to polarize, trigger, and break taboos. I rather mean that you are obliged to. There is no service to others like giving them the energetic food they need. Leaving the world as it is for the sake of "peace" is plain bullshit. Growth is happening through conflict and triggers, through friction and mistakes. What makes us suffer throughout these phases of friction is mostly merely the resistance to what is happening right now.

Throw away that old belief that so many of us still carry around with them: By taking your own space, you are taking from the others. This is not true. There is endless space, there is endless growth. By stepping into your space and into your full power, you are helping others to do the same. Editing yourself into a smaller version is damaging yourself and others, too.

When we think of a chameleon, it is the camouflaging aspect that comes to our mind at first. But a chameleon can also steer its eyes independently from each other, that means it can look at two different directions at the same time. There is no contradiction in feeling another one's suffering, inner conflicts, and issues but still holding your own space. You can do both: Not responding to another's expectations and still helping this person grow.

Rather than being rewarded with a clap on your head, you will be able to reward yourself with the most valuable thing in life: *freedom*.

About the Author

Solveig Berg, PhD. is a journalist, researcher, mother, housewife, money-hater, and system-dropout. Since 2019, she has been working as an online coach with women on the way of their inner calling.

With Conscious Reading, she is offering an online PhD training in reading and creating in the morphogenetic field, which is at the same time opening up the abilities of clairvoyance and clairsentience.

Solveig Berg was born in Germany but has been living in Sweden for more than ten years now with her two kids. To connect with Solveig, please check out her website: https://solveigberg.net/ or https://consciousreading.de

TRACY MAY

I Wasn't Crazy. He Was a Jerk!

As I sat crying, trapped in our car with him raging at me on our way to do something exciting (shop for new patio furniture), I couldn't help but feel broken. It happened again. He was screaming about everything under the sun.

I didn't know what set him off this time. What I did know is that I had made a "mistake" and stepped off the tightrope of living exactly how he expected me to, and he made me pay dearly for it as he verbally attacked me by calling me names, badgering me, accusing me of things I hadn't done.

I desperately wanted to be invisible and get away from him but opening the door while traveling 80 miles per hour on the highway didn't seem like the best solution.

As I stared out of the window for a moment to distract myself from the chaos, I caught a glimpse of a golf course. A memory rushed in of the moment we met on a golf course twenty years earlier and the instant connection we had. How I wished for that moment to return right then so we could go back to that feeling of love. I would have never imagined that I would end up here, 20 years later, feeling shattered in my third abusive relationship.

I was baffled by his anger, struggling to understand why he was so enraged. Desperate to stop his anger I defended myself. As he twisted everything I said, I screamed back hoping he'd listen to me. When reasoning with him didn't work, I sat in silence hoping he would quit roaring at me if I didn't respond, but he kept exploding at me until we got to our destination.

Two hours later, we pulled into the parking lot of the patio furniture store. I gathered myself as best as I could, stuffing down my pain and trauma, and calmly walked into the store as if nothing had happened and pretending to be fine.

We shopped for a couple of hours as I secretly held it together on pins and needles, dreading the drive home. Fortunately, we sat in silence for the 2-hour drive home, except for a few courteous exchanges of conversation which he initiated. He seemed calm and mild-mannered as he always did after he exploded at me.

I felt exhausted and spent. Like most nights, I crawled into bed fearing what tomorrow would bring.

This wasn't the first time he abused me, and it wouldn't be the last, but that night stands out as the start of the most abusive part of our relationship. That night, I started seriously considering ending my 17-year marriage and 20-year relationship.

Our love in the beginning was pure and beautiful, fun, and easy, much like everyone's. I felt free to be myself. I fell madly in love with this man who loved and enthralled me – an amazing change from my physically abusive ex-fiancé 6 years earlier. I thought I found my Prince Charming!

He moved in with me and my kids 8 months after meeting. Several months later, I was feeling suffocated. I brushed my feelings under the rug telling myself, "This is normal." I hadn't lived with a man in over six years.

A year later, we built our new home in the neighborhood that I dreamed of living in. Building the house was fun and frustrating as it is with all couples. Things went well until he ripped through the paint on the foyer wall after I mentioned a problem with the paint job. I felt scared but blamed his reaction on stress.

We had a beautiful wedding in our backyard 8 months later with our family and friends on what started as a calm and beautiful day that turned into what seemed like the windiest day ever! A sign from the universe?

We renewed our wedding vows on the beautiful beach of Jamaica while honeymooning - another dream come true. Life felt amazing.

Shortly after getting home, I put my 15-year software and accounting business on hold to start a business together. Our business strengths complemented each other perfectly so it made a lot of sense. Having a common goal drew us closer together as we worked hard growing our business. Things went smoothly for the most part as we forged a life together. Yet something felt off and I couldn't quite put my finger on it. There were more good times than bad at this point, so I shrugged the feeling off.

I distinctly remember the day that I realized his anger was a big problem. It was four years after we got married, we were driving to work together like we did every day. He suddenly became angry, yelling at other drivers, then he started yelling at me.

I hadn't put it together before that moment because I thought his angry episodes were isolated incidents. I began to reflect on many of our other fights in which I was blamed for doing something "wrong:" I moved plants in the landscaping, I exercised during our vacation, I went to bed after him. He'd get extremely upset about things most people wouldn't get angry about, but I didn't think of his anger as abusive at this point.

We didn't go from "dream come true" to falling apart all at once. His anger unraveled gradually over the course of our relationship; sporadic episodes here and there became every day raging by the end. Like a frog in a cold pot of water being slowly heated to boiling, I was increasingly conditioned to his anger over the life of our relationship without realizing it.

As the years progressed, any perceived slight became the basis for him to blow up. I instantly would become afraid of losing his love and go into damage control mode: explaining, justifying, trying to get him to understand my side and calm down. My attempts to curb his anger only enraged him even more and nothing was resolved.

With each passing year, I felt more and more like a crazy person, not knowing if Dr. Jekyll or Mr. Hyde would show up from moment to moment. I tiptoed around to avoid saying or doing anything that would set him off. What upset him one day wouldn't the next and vice versa. I never knew where I stood. Even when things were running smoothly, the threat of punishment was still looming over me. My body would feel tight as I constantly braced myself for the other shoe to drop.

In public, everyone saw him as a fun, generous, hardworking, loving guy who would do anything for you, and I experienced this side of him too. From the outside looking in, our life looked perfect.

In private, he seemed to erupt out of nowhere during a calm, normal conversation with me. Everything would change at the drop of a hat, and, before I realized it, he was suddenly exploding in anger, raging at me for something I said or did today, yesterday, last week, last month, last year, years ago or for something I might do or say in the future. Anything I did or said could and would be used against me later in FBI-like interrogations or twisted around in some fashion to make me question my sanity. I never knew when I'd be on the receiving end of his disapproval or punishment for not meeting his expectations.

I became extremely careful of what I said or did and who I spoke to as he would turn on a dime and go into crazy rages with accusations flying, asking where I was, who I was with, what I was doing. It felt like a full-on assault as he blamed me for his anger. I often felt like I had been beaten with a baseball bat after his verbal lashings.

In these moments, I felt lost and hopeless. The man standing before me was a stranger, he wasn't the loving, caring man I married. I wanted that man back.

At times, he was an entitled, controlling, selfish jerk that made me feel wrong for being me, triggering my deepest insecurity that I was broken and unlovable. Other times, he was loving, considerate, and caring. He would bring me flowers just to be nice. The dichotomy was enough to make me believe I was truly crazy.

I did everything I could to please him and to be a good wife and business partner. No matter what I did, nothing was ever good enough. He always found something to bully me about to make me feel small. I always felt so hurt and surprised by the depth of his meanness.

You think I would have gotten used to his unpredictable nature after so many years, but I didn't. I was always stunned by how he changed in an instant. And even though he had never hit me, I was scared of him and his reactions.

It hadn't always been like this. There were good times, even amazing times... that's why I stayed. But the good times grew less and less, and the abuse became more and more. I longed for the good times I had experienced with him like the time I was enjoying my 50th birthday "Gone with the Wind" party which he threw for me! I had an amazing dress made just for me and thoroughly enjoyed my guests and the fun. But inside, I was miserable, afraid I would do or say something that would trigger his next temper tantrum to criticize, blame, bully, badger, accuse me of cheating, whatever stoked his fury. And the accusations always came leaving me traumatized, shocked, and hurting. What happened to the man who adored me only a few moments ago at the party? How can he seem normal one moment and like a crazy lunatic the next?

I walked on eggshells every day, doing my best to keep the peace. I would experience calm for a day or two if I was lucky. If the calm lasted more than a week or two, I'd get hopeful. Then everything would come crashing down around me when his anger and frustration erupted even more than ever before, leaving me shattered, full of guilt and shame because everything was my fault.

Little by little, year by year, I started shutting down, pulling away from him. There was no safe space emotionally or physically.

He'd read my journal and searched my phone without my permission, twisting my words to mean I was cheating. "I liked to dance" was in my profile in a women's group I belonged to and that meant I was "looking for guys" even though my profile also said I was married, a mom, and a grandma.

I no longer felt safe to share my dreams, desires, wants, needs, excitements, fears, or hurts. Everything was used as a weapon against me. I stopped living and started surviving.

More than once he stood outside the locked bathroom door for hours raging at me. "You're a whore!" he would scream while accusing me of screwing all the men in my investment group. "You didn't approve the application for the client? How could you be so stupid!" he blasted at me. "You don't love me! All you want is my money!" he exploded searching for any crazy reason he could justify to badger me.

Navigating his roller coaster of emotions became my full-time job. My life revolved around managing his anger. Getting up in the mornings became a challenging task as I wanted to avoid him as much as possible. Exhausted and overwhelmed was now my norm. I doubted and second-guessed myself frequently. My life was turned upside down, and I didn't know how to turn it upright.

I was living a personal hell I didn't even know how to explain myself – let alone to anyone else. There were no bruises, no broken bones, no holes in the wall or broken dishes. How do you explain this craziness to another person? It felt so unreal that I didn't have words to define it. And there was no way that I could share any of this when I was seen by everyone as a strong, confident, successful mom, woman, businesswoman; and I was... everywhere except in my relationship.

I woke up in the middle of the night in 2013, acutely aware that our marriage had eroded to where I was beat down nearly every day. Not physically, but verbally, emotionally and psychologically. I was at a point where I had lost all sense of myself and my self-confidence. I was so desperate to end the emotional pain inside of me that I didn't want to live anymore. I contemplated suicide often to end my pain. I knew deep down it wasn't normal to feel like this, so I'd push the thought away.

I was convinced his anger was all my fault. And I must be the problem. Afterall, he was only angry with me and no one else. If only I could figure out a way to stop his anger.

That night finally led me to look for answers to my suffering other than therapy (which wasn't working). Therapy helped me get through the rough patches, but it didn't stop the abuse. For years, I bought relationship programs, books, audios, attended relationship events – you name it, I tried it! I did everything that I could to fix what was wrong with me that caused his anger. We tried couples counseling and couples therapy events, but he'd twist everything around until the therapist believed I was the problem, or he'd talk about work during our sessions.

I can't explain why I didn't leave years ago. From the outside looking in, it looked like a no-brainer to anyone. I should have left. I wanted to salvage our relationship and was determined to do whatever it took to fix us. We had a marriage, a history, a life that I did not want to believe was wasted. We had a dream home, sports cars, wonderful vacations, a successful business, healthy and successful kids. We had success everywhere but in our relationship. I desperately wanted success there, too.

If I am honest with myself, the bad far outweighed the good at this point, especially emotionally. I was hooked into the potential of who he could be, believing his promises and the possibility of how great our relationship could be. After all, our relationship really was great at times. I knew deep down that I should end the marriage, but I just couldn't. I loved him – the *good* part of him. I wanted that part of him back all the time.

I felt like I was living in a minefield most days. Every time I cleared one mine, new mines came up out of nowhere, from every direction, exploding in my face: going to Target alone to pick up a few things, going to lunch with my adult daughter (just us girls), horseback riding lessons with my granddaughter, a bike ride on my own or using a different gift bag for my kids instead of his. These were all "mines" that detonated leaving behind a wake of destruction and devastation. Simply wanting to go on a three-day fitness adventure out of town with my online women's fitness group caused another explosion. Visiting my brother and his family for a week or traveling to see my sister for a few days brought out the "landmine squad."

He would badger me for days or weeks on end, however long it took, to pressure me to change my mind, and I almost always did. It was easier to give in. He would make sure I paid a hefty price for "excluding" him. And days, weeks, months, years later, I would be attacked during a tirade for how I "wanted" to go anywhere without him, even if he went with me. Double standards were the norm with him as he could golf whenever he wanted to and do whatever he wanted without me.

In 2015, I was still living in a battlefield day in and day out when I finally had all I could take. I got the courage to leave, hoping the anger would stop. It didn't. He became even more volatile, so I moved back after a month to de-escalate his anger.

Discouraged, I thought, *I am a smart woman, why can't I figure this out! Why isn't anything I try working?*

Desperate to find a solution, I went to a 5-day inner-child healing intensive hoping to finally find answers. I discovered how destructive being abandoned by my dad at three and raised by my alcoholic mom and abusive alcoholic stepdad was to my beliefs and relationship patterns. The abandonment, neglect, and S.H.I.T. (Shame, Hurt, Insecurities, Trauma) I experienced as a child set me up to seek familiar dynamics unconsciously in intimate relationships.

Anger, emotional disconnection, breadcrumbs of love felt familiar and safe subconsciously even though I longed for peace, connection, and love. I uncovered that I had codependent beliefs that sabotaged my relationships because deep down I felt broken, not enough, unlovable. I thought the key to saving my marriage was stopping his anger, no clue healing my beliefs was significant.

I discovered my need to get him to stop abusing me came from not feeling safe or loved in my childhood, a belief that if I could get love from others, then I would be safe. And that is just what I did as an adult; tried to get love from every unavailable man I could find, who was just like my mom, step-dad, and dad combined.

It all made perfect sense.

I finally had my "aha moment." I unconsciously endured abuse to get the love I didn't get in my childhood and accepted the breadcrumbs of love he offered between abusive episodes to get the love I craved to feel lovable. I discovered I had no power to make him stop abusing me. He wouldn't change unless he wanted to. What a mind-blowing breakthrough! And a terrifying one. If I couldn't get him to change, he would never stop abusing me. Then how do I fix us?

I used the process from the intensive to work on my beliefs daily. As the months went by, I was clearing childhood beliefs, finding the real me, and healing my patterns. But he remained unchanged; he was still raging and abusing me almost daily despite claiming he wanted to change.

Most days, I felt like I was taking one step forward and two steps back. My need to end his anger was undeterred. It honestly felt like an addiction. I literally could not give up no matter how bad things got. I clung to my belief he loved me and would eventually stop abusing me.

As I frantically kept searching for answers to hold my life together, I discovered information about narcissists. Intrigued as some pieces fit the puzzle, I researched more, and the more I explored, I saw myself, my husband, my relationships, and my childhood in those pages and videos over and over.

As I uncovered more about narcissists, I could finally put a name to the craziness I had been experiencing for years. I now had words to describe my suffering: circular conversations, gaslighting, control, manipulation, lack of empathy, entitlement, love bombing, hoovering, idealization, devalue, and discarding.

I realized that my husband was likely a narcissist (a taker), and I was an empath (a giver). This was my light bulb moment! Thank God! Hallelujah! Things began to make sense. I wasn't crazy after all!

A sense of relief and peacefulness came over me. I began to feel hopeful for the first time in many years. It wasn't all my fault. And that relief came and went, back and forth, as I tried hard to wrap my head around this concept of narcissism.

Just when I would start to understand it all and believe it was him and not me, he would act loving and caring, and I would go back to doubting myself.

I was still making excuses for his anger as I held tight onto my denial of how terrible life had become. Avoiding the truth was easy. "He hadn't hit me," I rationalized. "Maybe it wasn't that bad. I just needed to try harder." All the knowledge in the world wasn't helping me.

Late in 2016, I finally reached my breaking point. I couldn't take one more moment of abuse and crazy conversations. I hit rock bottom and was desperate to get my life back. I finally admitted to myself I needed help to get unstuck from the craziness of my marriage, so I hired a coach. Best decision ever.

She helped me start loving myself and challenge my beliefs and co-dependency patterns that I had developed in childhood. For the first time in an intimate relationship, I actually kept boundaries and made my needs important. As I implemented what my coach taught me, taking more responsibility for myself and my needs, and stopped accepting the blame and abuse, things got much worse to my surprise.

His anger escalated, turning to physical abuse: throwing things, standing in front of me while blocking my path or the door-way, standing over me while yelling at me. Following me and threatening me when I walked away from his raging became part of his intimidation tactic. His intensifying anger felt like my worst nightmare. My relationship was supposed to get better with coach-ing, not worse!

Luckily when I felt hopeless and wanted to quit, when I felt afraid to keep making these changes, I had my coach on my side pulling me through it. She'd guide me back to what I wanted: love, peace, and connection, and I was able to keep going.

As I continued making changes within me, things escalated to the point that he pushed and grabbed me a couple of times, he even grabbed my neck once attempting to stop me from walking away. That was it, my final straw, a boundary I would not let him violate. I demanded he move out.

He tried every trick in the book to get me back - Hoovering (sucking me back in with promises of changing, extreme remorsefulness, apologizing, even threatening self-harm, whatever it took to get me back). Then he'd go back to Love Bombing (showering me with love, excessive affection, attention, flattery, praise, flowers, the charming person I fell in love with would appear talking about our future, the anger and abuse disappeared).

He would come to work so dejected by our separation, making it even harder to stay the course because of the entanglement of our business. My income and assets were intertwined with him and our business. Even though I was 50% owner, he'd threatened to take everything or lose everything just to spite me when I suggested divorce. I wasn't 23, pregnant, leaving my 1st husband, nor was I 29 leaving my ex-fiancé. I was in my 50's and scared about my future.

I wasn't scared to be alone; I was terrified of losing his love. He'd suddenly become the loving man he used to be when we were separated, and I let him move back weeks or months later. When we were separated the suffering and fear was so intense that it felt like I was having withdrawals, which is Trauma Bonds. Rinse and repeat this cycle for two exhausting years.

For 3 years, I battled to heal my patterns, beliefs, and trauma that kept me stuck in abusive relationships my whole life. I fought hard to break free from our cycle and to believe in and trust myself. He fought hard to keep me in the cycle and to maintain control of me.

At times, I was able to hold my boundaries no matter his reaction; other times, I gave in, too scared of losing his love to stand up for myself. I worried he would change for the next person and she would get what I wanted. Despite my fears and having to deal with him constantly fighting me, my coach helped me continue on my path. Even when I wavered, I always came back to choosing me and stepping out of the cycle of abuse.

As I struggled on my journey, I slowly began to love and accept myself and feel safe to be me again. Once I was able to give myself the love and safety I needed, I broke the cycle of toxicity. I was finally confident enough to stop being his punching bag for the sake of saving our relationship. The key, I discovered, is self-love that recognizes unloving patterns in myself and others.

As I got stronger within, unwilling to compromise myself or my values, he started to change. His anger deescalated. The abusive episodes became less frequent, and the intensity of his anger decreased, which felt great. Even though the abuse became almost tolerable, it didn't completely stop. Any abuse was now intolerable because I recognized that I deserved better. I knew it was time to let go and love myself enough to move on to a life of healthy love and support. As painful as I knew it would be, I had to put myself and my wellbeing first. I was ready to file for divorce. It wasn't an easy journey, but it definitely was worth it!

I am here today to say from experience and my journey if you feel something is off in your relationship, something is. Even if you're not being physically abused, you might be emotionally, verbally, psychologically, financially, or sexually abused. Abuse can be very covert and unnoticeable. Psychological abuse is very insidious and destructive to your soul and wellbeing. Often you don't realize you're being abused because you're being blamed for the abuser's anger. I didn't realize I was being abused for a very long time. Here are some key takeaways I discovered:

- I didn't cause nor can I stop his anger.
- Emotional and psychological abuse is just as damaging as physical abuse.
- The absence of physical abuse doesn't mean I'm not being abused.
- When something feels off, trust myself.
- Reach out for help because I couldn't do it on my own.

I have been where you are, in the midst of the turmoil and uncertainty, fighting for my sanity, wanting to desperately save my relationship and get the love back. I was loving the good part of him, hating the abusive part of him, all while losing myself.

Because of what I went through, I understand on a very deep level. I don't want you to have to go through years of suffering, confusion, helplessness, and hopelessness, struggling to figure it all out like I did. It is possible to go from barely surviving to thriving, even if it feels impossible right now.

I am passionate about helping you know you don't deserve to live this way. You deserve a life filled with love, happiness, and healthy relationships and all life has to offer. There is a better way, and that is to get help now. You are not meant to do it alone.

I now help women rise from the ashes of toxic love every day to have joyful relationships full of love and support through one-on-one and group Toxic Love Recovery coaching programs. Coaching changed my life forever, and I know it can change yours, too.

I couldn't do my journey alone, and neither should you. Sign up for your complimentary "Heal Your Heart Breakthrough Session" and uncover your next steps to getting the life and love you deserve.

I can't wait for you to finally be free, too!

About the Author

Tracy May is a Toxic Love Recovery Specialist and Women's Empowerment Coach who overcame adversity in a childhood full of trauma and abuse. Not only has she been in the trenches of three abusive relationships as an adult, but she freed herself of the limiting beliefs that kept her stuck in one for over 20 years. During her transformation from surviving to thriving, she realized she wanted to help women who are suffering as she had, who feel broken, invisible, and unlovable to re-discover their true worth and lovability, so they feel free to be themselves and have the relationship they have always craved.

Her discoveries on her journey of healing and uncovering her true self guide her to empower women to break free from the chains of toxic love and the limiting beliefs that keep them stuck accepting breadcrumbs for love.

Tracy's certifications in several modalities support her to empower women all over the world just like you to finally have the relationship and the life they dream of.

Tracy's unique perspective to help female entrepreneurs break free from toxic love while building their empire originates in her experience of building three successful businesses while raising two kids on her own despite the chaos and confusion in her personal life from toxic relationships.

When Tracy isn't coaching, you can find her soaking up the sun at home or on a beach getaway, horseback riding, golfing and relishing time with her two children, five grandchildren and one great-granddaughter.

Tracy fiercely believes in you and her loving, warm, and compassionate nature shines through while she supports you in conquering the entanglement of abuse.

Tracy offers Heal Your Heart Breakthrough Sessions to start your journey of healing. Schedule your Complimentary **Heal Your Heart** Session at: http://www.talkwithtracymay.com

To connect with Tracy, please visit:

Website: https://www.fiercelyempowered.com

Facebook group: https://www.facebook.com/groups/breakfree-fromtoxiclove/

Instagram: https:/instagram.com/break_free_from_toxic_love/

TikTok: https://www.tiktok.com/@gaslighting_wth

Linkedin: https://linkedin.com/in/tracy-may1

U-Tube: https://www.youtube.com/channel/UC-7L-DAhk6X1smrWQ7Y_U9w

VIVIAN SHAPIRO

Free to Be Vibrant Me

Poem by: Vivian Shapiro, January 2022

I had a vision

that Vibrance came to me,

and this is what she whispered in my ear:

"I am Vibrance.

Who am I?

I am one, and I am many

ignited by flames of visions

Of visualisations

Of verve and vitality

Loving to dance and frolic

in the colours of life,

I breathe in intensity

I breathe out passion.

I'm authentically alive!

I live with and through

both pain and pleasure.

In the playgrounds of positivity,

I sensually seize each day.

I will refresh you...

Help you feel resilient

Help you feel alive with

love,

life,

light,

and

laughter.

I offer invitations

to all

to drink a full glass

of my sweet sensation.

Stir it soulfully

So you may be fulfilled

by its magical secrets."

Fortunately, I listened well!

When things are meant to be

There it was yet again. That phrase: "I want to be you when I grow up!" followed by the question, "Viv, how do you do it? Where do you get that energy? And how do you stay so vibrant?" I was reconnecting with a friend and teacher that I had hired over fifteen years ago. After engaging in a very lively discussion, Robyn looked into my eyes and added, "No really, Viv! I want to know. What is your secret sauce?" Of course, I was flattered.

People have commented on my vibrancy many times throughout my life, and fortunately, I am still getting comments like this even at 76 years old. This time was different. I didn't just slough it off, giggle, and thank the person modestly. I stated excitedly and boldly (and quite loudly I might add), "I am going to find out!" I think my friend thought I had truly lost my mind.

That evening, I went into a deep and serious self-study. I needed to find out the answer to my questions:

- Why do people say that to me?
- Who am I?
- What am I still meant to do?
- What is it that I do, portray, emulate, magnify, project to others that have had these kinds of phrases uttered to me repetitively?

I made a list of the most common phrases that come my way, and I share these here somewhat shyly but paradoxically immodestly, for the moment.

When flattering comments come your way

- *I want to be you when I grow up!*
- *I wish I had your energy.*
- *You pick me up.*
- *I'm inspired by watching you.*
- *How do you always see the strengths in others – even in those that have treated you wrongly?*
- *You always manage to have a positive attitude!*
- *You light up a room.*
- *I love how you always come up with solutions.*
- *You are the eternal optimist.*
- *You saved my life!*
- *You remind me of Goldie Hawn!*

Yes, all these utterances to me are indeed very flattering and quite lovely. What is it that I did or continue to do to deserve such high praise and recognition? What exactly is it that I do or have done to live with a positive, forward-moving mindset? How have I lived my life to present myself as this person that others want to emulate?

Other than weakly acknowledging my strengths, I have allowed my eyes to focus on my weaknesses. I have succumbed to my own view of myself as insecure, needy, self-deprecating, compulsive, definitely type A, a perfectionist, sometimes controlling, and even a bit bitchy. I also know that I can be too much for some people – much too much. Jealousy and intimidation have led envious colleagues and acquaintances to bully me or create falsehoods and untrue rumours about me. Thank goodness that's only a small percentage, and the truth is, it's their loss. They missed out having a true, loyal, fun-loving, and supportive friend that would go to the ends of the earth for them!

Many friends, family, and acquaintances have tried to open my eyes to those aspects that humble me, fill my heart with love, and make me realise that I have "some 'splaining to do," as Ricky would often say to Lucy! I was now ready to honour me and explain proudly.

I was up for the task; I was ready to plunge into the core of me to discover what I was truly all about. What were the characteristics, the attributes that made me stand out as *vibrant* to others? What was my secret sauce? Correction: What IS my secret sauce?

These questions propelled me to enter the doorway to my stash of over forty journals. Started over 40 years ago, their covers have more colours than Joseph's coat! My journals are my best friends. They allow me to say or tell stories about anything! They don't judge; they do not receive marks for literary prowess, and best of all, they don't answer back (although sometimes I answer back)!

Writing in a journal, for me, was how I made promises to myself, where I allowed my deepest thoughts and feelings to erupt with no real intention other than to release my truths and to look back and see if I did indeed do what I hoped to achieve or advised myself to do.

Different from my pre-teen and teenage journals which contained mostly gossip and information on my latest crushes or BFF adventures, writing in my adult journals was a way for me to bring my adventures to life, make honest comments about events and to bring my artistic skills to the fore, especially that of my poetic self. Truthfully and sadly, I had not spent much time checking in with my past self that was speaking to my future self. However, my journal writing continues to this day, albeit in many changed formats. The good news? I saved them ALL! I decided it was now time to dedicate myself to pouring myself into my words and re-living my truths.

I couldn't wait to venture down the multi-coloured road of "Journal Land" to find my VIBRANT SELF and discover the MAGIC of ME (and whatever other things I would uncover). Gleefully, I went on this journey with my highlighters, sticky notes, and my backpack full of additional questions:

- *Have I learned from past experiences?*
- *Had I met my intended goals?*
- *Had I followed up on promises I made to myself?*
- *Had I listened to my own advice?*

Perhaps there was more of a purpose to these forty plus notebooks of various sizes and shapes than to take up so much room that I had to find a special IKEA unit to house them along with my many photo albums. Perhaps I could find something worth sharing with the world. Perhaps there was a gift in the many words and thoughts poured into these pages that might help someone find their truer self. I was about to find out.

When looking at yourself through objective eyes

Before me lay a combination of tender, heartbreaking, happy, angry, sensitive stories of every kind of genre and subject, my own personal thoughts on living, learning, and loving in a variety of forms. My journals were beautiful, sad, angry, funny, clever. They contained poems, both rhyming and free verse, ideas for songs, rough drafts of songs that actually made it on billboard, "Vivianisms" (my unique sayings), sketches, drawings, favourite lines from songs, personal paintings, and portraits when the mood struck me.

I was stunned when I read through them. I was surprisingly impressed at my writing ability and sensitivity. My words, even to this day as I continue to write, are written without thought to grammar, spelling, meaning but just flow. As I dove deep into my journals, keeping my modesty in my back pocket, I congratulated myself on how perceptive they were and are.

I did find a number of qualities of mine that stood out no matter the content, my family craziness, my challenges with life, my exuberant moments, or my angry bitter experiences. I realised

I could fill up the letters of VIBRANT to create an acronym, and oh, how I love acronyms!

Throughout many of my stumbling blocks and challenges, whether they were family, relationship, health, or other, I found out that even in my lowest moments and deepest of funks, I focused on remaining...

V a Visionary with Vitality

I an Inspirer and Influencer

B a Bold Bosslady

R a Resilient Romantic

A an Action-Oriented Achiever

N a Nurturing soul, searching her own Nirvana

T a Tenacious Trailblazer grateful for her Tribe

I was VIBRANT with experiences full of many loves, losses, and lessons! That's when the book that I was meant to write appeared to me in a vision! The timing was perfect.

When a vision becomes clear

At the very moment that I was actually contemplating having something to offer others, revealing my secret sauce while leaving a legacy for my family, I was contacted by a self-publishing school to take a look at their courses and coaching. *How did they know? The universe!* After receiving a 45-minute free workshop on the possibilities, I realised that this publishing school and my learning modality were a match! The support, coaching and lessons offered to a newbie author aligned with what I was looking for. This was the Law of Attraction in action!

I envisioned a book that would capture my joie de vivre, (actually my "joie de **VIV**-re!") capitalising on a potpourri of my adventures and stories in no necessary chronological order that would depict a life of VIBRANCY, of verve and vitality no matter the circumstances. I imagined my purpose and my intention would be to make the most of who and what I was to serve myself, my family and my community to the best of my ability. I now had answers and stories I was ready to share. I knew these stories would be strictly from my own truths and perspectives and perhaps others would have different versions. Nonetheless, I believed I had a mission to share my experiences.

I envisioned the title:

Living a VIBRANT Life (or "Go Vibrant")

Notes on learning, leasing, loving, and lavishing the "joie de VIV-re"! *(or something like that, still to be decided)*

And thus, a potential book and a new budding author was born, labour pains and all. I had many moments of imposter syndrome wondering: *'Who am I to write a book to tell others how to live?'* I then realised I was not "telling others" anything. McDonald's claim to fame in the 70's was their Big Mac with a clever tongue-twisting jingle commercial of *"two all-beef patties, special sauce, lettuce, cheese, pickles, onions, and a sesame seed bun."* The jingle hit the airwaves, and everyone was singing it or attempting to have success with this tongue twister. Today, we would declare that it went viral! It was the customer's choice however whether to engage in the whole experience. I envisioned that I would offer my special sauce ingredients and an invitation to bite into my vibrant hamburger. It would be the readers' choice whether to top it up with all the fixings or not!

I wrote this to myself to value and honour my right of passage into the world of literacy. I am a lover of life, an observer of opportunities, a scriber of stories, an editor of experiences, a singer of songs, a ponderer of poetry, an empath of everything, a feeler of fantasies, a masseuse of messages, a teacher of thoughts, a dealer of dreams. I am in fact just like you. I am an ordinary person with ordinary experiences yet extraordinary messages that may help one find strategies for a happy, joyful, engaging and authentic *you*. I help others live a life you control, a life in which you will be empowered to rise above no matter the entanglements.

Revisiting the moment you released the vibrant you

I ran into the house, locked the door and shed the tears welling deep inside of me. I was a mess. I knew what I had to do! It was time. But first I needed someone to lean on.

I called my girlfriend at midnight, but when she picked up the phone I could barely speak. Without hesitation, she said, "It sounds like you could use some emotional support." As a true good friend is bound to do, she met me at Tim Hortons, her pajamas still on underneath her spring jacket. We sipped on our steaming coffee as she helped me unload my hurting heart. May 26, 1994, will be forever etched in my mind as the day I unlocked my cage. Sharon B. sat and listened compassionately as I spoke. It is amazing that she even understood me as the words were muffled by heavy sobs, tears flowing down my reddened eyes.

Earlier that day, I had been looking forward to our Annual Principals' Dinner Dance Event. Sharon and I were going together without spouses. Mine was at a nearby conference and unavailable and hers disliked that sort of thing. Fine! We were a great bonded, congenial group of colleagues who knew how to work hard and play hard, and though spouses and partners were definitely invited and included, some chose to come solo.

My husband changed his mind at the last minute, calling to say he had decided to come home to attend with me. I really was not sure why this sudden change of mind, as he was adamant the day before that he could not and would not be there! With this news, Sharon decided to stay home. I pretended I was thrilled at this sudden change; however, something was telling me to say "No, don't come!" What was that line from *Pretty Woman* that Miss Vivian said to the high fashion store clerks? "BIG MISTAKE... BIG! HUGE!" Yes Miss Viv! "BIG MISTAKE!" I should have listened to my instincts. But then the rest would not have happened. And it was meant to.

The event itself was fabulous but for me it was a disaster. The evening became a battleground for what was already a dysfunctional relationship. My husband was angry for whatever reasons unbeknownst to me. I was blamed for choosing to sit with colleagues of mine that talked shop and for a host of other reasons as to why he thought I was not a good wife. We usually looked like a happy, well-balanced couple on the dance floor and that is where I led him. I assumed that emotions would fade away while we danced...they did not.

In a louder than normal voice, many accusatory hurtful words were said to me, right in the middle of the dance floor. I could see by the look of pity in the eyes of one of my colleagues dancing nearby how sad she was for me. I excused myself and went to the bathroom in an attempt to regain my composure. My friend who witnessed my unhappiness came to see how I was, hugged me, and said, "Oh Vivian, you of all people don't deserve that!" This was my final WAKE UP call! And I answered, "Thank you, Bev. You are absolutely right!"

I asked her if she wouldn't mind going into the event area to tell my husband that I was waiting in the car to go home. As I gathered my things from the dinner table to make my quiet departure, I felt others' quizzical eyes on me, wondering why their lively, social, "dance-til-the-music-stops" colleague was retiring so early. I couldn't even look at anybody. The pain of embarrassment was too great.

When he opened the car door, I had already detached myself. Thus, this driver of the car was given cool, unemotional instructions to take me straight home and to go back to his %#@## Conference if he wished. Somehow in that moment, I grew strong. Despite my insides being torn asunder, my mind was clear and calm, full of courage and conviction.

At the coffee shop later, Sharon offered me the strength I needed to pause, breathe and reflect. I confessed that I could not take the hurt anymore. She acknowledged my pain and affirmed my value as a person. It may seem like a small incident, but it was unfortunately one of too many occurrences of our declining marriage. I was done. I felt unappreciated and undervalued. Though once again, my heart was broken, my vision was suddenly fixed! No one could define my worth but me. Here I was after many unhappy years, ready to get out of this pattern of concession and set myself free. I would emerge from my cocoon as the beautiful vibrant butterfly I knew I could be, ready to spread my wings. I was beckoned to fly higher into a better space.

I slept well that night, prepared for what I knew my decision would be the next day. I was prepared to step into my power and reclaim responsibility for my happiness! Until...I woke up with Debbie Doubt lying right beside me! She entered my mind and soul and I immediately jumped into my "insecurity" role. Feeling guilty about not having had more compassion or support for my husband surrounded by my colleagues and all their "shop talk," I decided to apologize and left him a message at his office to call

325

me. We were married for 28 years, a lot to give up! Yes, I was running around that familiar track yet again, still hoping for things to change along the way.

However, it was no coincidence that as soon as I drove out of the driveway for work, the radio was blaring the lyrics of "I Will Survive" by Gloria Gaynor. These lyrics spoke to me loud and clear:

"It took all the strength I had not to fall apart

Kept trying hard to mend the pieces of my broken heart

And I spent oh-so many nights just feeling sorry for myself

I used to cry, but now I hold my head up high

And you see me, somebody new,

I'm not that chained up little person still in love with you..."

And I knew that I too would survive! I needed to forget how I felt and remember what I deserved. My heart was finally accepting what my mind already knew. By the end of the song, my mind was made up. I was running my victory lap, the last one and getting prepared for the celebration ahead. Debbie Doubt had left the building for good!

At 11AM his call was put through to my principal's office. I simply said, "I want you to know, I'm calling a mediator recommended to me. I will see you at home. I have to go, I'm busy." And that was the beginning of the end and a start to the new and improved me.

As sad as I was, I felt a great weight being lifted from my mind, body and soul. I saw it as a new chapter for me! What would

ENTANGLED NO MORE

I call this new life? I quickly wrote in my journal what this chapter might be called in my imaginary book:

Free to be Vibrant Me

Goodbye at Last

Feeling Elated

Relieved and Rejuvenated

A Heavy Burden Lightened

Flying Higher

Empowered to Be Me

It's a New Start

Energized

Lightening My Load

Feeling Empowered

Unentangled

I knew it would not be easy, but one thing I knew was I was staying true to myself, honouring me!

Here is the poem I wrote two days later:

Finding Vivian

Freedom at last

A break from the past

No more words that rip apart

No surging pain upon my heart

The truth was told

A decision bold

Made clear with fear and trepidation

Yet what I feel is pure elation

No more questions no accusing

No more hurtful word-abusing

Free oh yes so free am I

Should I feel this good, this high?

I know I'll come down very soon

Amidst the family life now ruined

I only hope that what I have done

Will leave no damage to my sons

I'm ready to take my new life on

Living alone now where I belong

Finding myself, being true to me

I'm free, I'm free My God ... I'm free

Vivian Shapiro, May 28, 1994

May 28, 1994. The start of a new day, a new life. I admit I was terrified.

When seeking help fails…

I honestly don't know what happened in the 28 years together, but we did not work anymore. Our relationship was more than dysfunctional. It was sad…very sad, because I believe that we really did love each other.

Life wasn't always maladaptive. We were a very handsome couple in the late 1960s and onward for quite a few years. We were very sociable, adventurous, adoring each other, proud and loving parents of two delicious boys who were an absolute treat. We were travellers, homeowners, cottage owners, ambitious in our own fields of work, successful, music lovers, car fanatics, concert goers, jive dance contest winners, and the list goes on. But we were both unhappy.

We tried therapy before this. They say if even a small ember exists in that heap of wood, which might ignite by fanning it, you should try to see if the fire can be restarted. Our therapist stated: "You two are like a golden Cadillac. You look good, all stylish and classy, but when you open the hood the motor doesn't work!" (If it were today, he'd call it a Tesla with no charger!) I personally think it was so broken, it likely would not even be picked up for a used car lot! Ready for the junkyard it was.

Therapy only helps when there are no lies told. Therapy only helps when each person is careful not to manipulate the conversation. Therapy only helps when each person plays authentically and is willing to see their own areas for improvement.

Therapy only helps when you truly madly deeply want things to change. Therapy is not about blaming; it is about finding ways together that will aid in repairing, restoring, and renewing, writing a clean slate based on love and respect. Our motor was beyond repair, ego was our fuel and thus the guidelines were not always adhered to.

We separated very soon after the dinner dance evening and both our lives took on a whole new chapter in two vastly different books. The next two years were brutal for me. I became easily depressed when alone and found myself in "no person's land", an island unto myself. I was fortunate to have very supportive staff, friends and a close family. I did remain true to my promise to look after myself and shine my worth once more!

When you recognize you have a gift

The book I will soon present to the world is a slice of my soul. There are lessons learned from the stories in my journals that I have been writing since I was 35 years old! My promise to myself after our separation was to live a full, blessed and treasured life where I valued not only my family and friends but through consistent and conscious intention, I would live a vibrant full-on life.

I had a gift, and I was unwrapping it slowly. This gift presented itself to my close friends and work colleagues, yet unfortunately, it was a gift that, in the presence of my husband, was left tightly wrapped up in a dark closet, seeing the light only in his absence. I vowed to never leave it lonely and unwanted again.

What was in my package? One of the items was my inherent character of positivity. My apologies to my readers if I sound like I am bragging and definitely being immodest. Through my most hurting times, I allowed my positivity to break down the "tough times" or "poor me" wall. I focused on my gift. I brought clarity to my thoughts on the fact that my husband and I had lots of good years and brought into this life two very amazing now adult males with many talents and abilities to offer the world. My gift was not always appreciated by my spouse, and perhaps there were other gifts that would suit him better. He could find a new car with a motor that worked with his chassis. Me too. While I wasn't in any rush at all to look for that new car with a humming motor, I knew, in time, there would be one special edition out there, probably in the used car lot, given up by an unappreciative owner, that would suit my style, with a driver that would adore me as co-driver. (Turns out there was!)

During my early years of separation, I started to realize bit by bit the gift I had to pass onto others. I tried to remain unplugged and started to listen to only affirming and acknowledging words. My aperture opened. I vowed to make better choices. Where focus goes, energy flows. My focus would be intentional. I would not allow myself to get entangled in someone else's insecurities and problems. I was ready to glow with the flow. I vowed to create a new movement and lead with life, my values, my dreams, my vision. And I didn't need a man to do it!

I invite you to unwrap the gift I have carefully tied with a glorious ribbon to find the hidden gifts in you. Some of the items in this box are:

Laughter

Humour

Seeing the strengths in others

Authenticity

Energy

Acceptance

Resilience

Courage

When knowing there is still more for you to do

I am excited about my upcoming book. I hope to influence others' lives as an intentional impactor and an agent for change. I act with courage to care about myself enough to do things in the higher level of consciousness to release fear, anger, and apathy knowing these do not serve me.

I knew I needed to activate my light, not only for myself, but for others. I will model what's possible. I knew that if I could fulfil my potential, then I could show others how to do so. I want my readers to cry and laugh along with me and some of my adventures and experiences with the belief that they can purposefully bring on a VIBRANT life no matter their age or circumstances. I can't wait to start the journey with others who vie to be truly "entangled no more!"

Showing Up in the Now

Poem by: Vivian Shapiro, October 2021

My 75th year will soon pass me by
As my 76th is now drawing nigh.
Been quite the year with stress and strife
Surviving through fears in this COVID life.
Am I getting old? Hey, wait! NOT ME!
I still think and act like at least 33!
As I watch autumn leaves that gently fall,
I think of transitions that happen to all.
Through my personal changes, I've shown up big,
Discarding those leaves that no longer give
My life, it's true purpose. I'll reveal the now!
Uncovering each day, my why, what, and how.
I have much to give, more to love, this I know.
Spread my power and magic with more room to grow.
Today, I choose "moi" and accept what will be
Everything, yes, everything, is RIGHT about ME!

Dear Reader,

Please know, everything is also right about you! Everything! Much of your ability and actions to help you live vibrantly, away from entanglements that keep you tightly wound up like a ball of yarn, are waiting eagerly, ready to be unraveled into a beautifully knitted, woven piece of art. Thank you for reading Free to Be Vibrant Me! This chapter was a small slice of the notes, anecdotes and antidotes I share with you, the reader, in my soon-to-be-launched solo book* to engage those of you wishing to create a life of vibrance. In those chapters, I take you to an outer space journey through the V.I.B.R.A.N.T. galaxy as we travel to stars representing each letter that signify words or actions representing each letter! Join me as I share the secret sauce for my "joie de VIV-re" with the hope I may influence your desire to reach that universe too!

Lokah Samastah Sukhino Bhavantu is a Sanskrit Mantra to radiate the feeling of love and happiness towards the world:

"May all beings everywhere be happy and free,
and may the thoughts, words, and actions of my own life
contribute in some way to that happiness and to that freedom for all."

Thank you all.

You are beautiful and loved and vibrant!

About the Author

Vivian Shapiro is an energetic, positive-minded influencer, blessed and grateful to be highly active and vibrant at 75+ years, living a life that is far from over!

She is thrilled to be a contributing author of Entangled No More in which she gives a preview into her upcoming solo book. It relates the moment she knew she could turn her painful existence into a "joie de VIV-re" power.

A former Toronto teacher, vice principal, and principal, Vivian's achievements go well beyond the school system. For twenty years after retirement, as the Education Director for the Herbert H. Carnegie Future Aces Foundation, she spearheaded programs and conferences to empower disenfranchised youth. Vivian was hailed as a servant leader when she received the 2012 Amazing Aces in Action Award and the 2018 "Celebrating Outstanding Women Award" for Philanthropy.

Creativity abounds in Vivian's list of accomplishments. She has co-written three songs, one a universal message of hope and peace. She is a writer of in-house children's books, plays, poetry, retirement party and conference scripts, creator of a children's show co-hosted with her grandson, artistic director, singer, actress, dancer, choreographer, a wedding officiant, and a clubhouse room moderator to name a few.

As mom to a blended five families, she loves engaging as "vava" to her thirteen grandchildren. As Regional Vice President with Arbonne International, a certified B Corporation company, focusing on clean, safe plant-based products, she coaches and trains people to create a life of choice and abundance. Vivian has a passion to help others defy aging by immersing themselves in a healthy lifestyle no matter gender or age. Her mission is to teach others to create new habits and opportunities that will serve them a lifetime of vibrancy.

Check her website for the launching of her first solo book this fall on tips to live a vibrant life! If you would like to connect with Vivian, the links are below.

Linktree: https://www.vivianshapiro.com/links/

Website: https://www.vivianshapiro.com

Biz: https://www.arbonne.com/ca/en/arb/vivandamanda

ABOUT SOULFUL VALLEY PUBLISHING

International best-selling author, Katie Carey, created the Soulful Valley Publishing House in May 2021. Katie is the host of the Soulful Valley Podcast ranking globally in the Top 0.5%. Katie uses both the podcast and the multi-author books as a platform to help metaphysical coaches, energy healers, authors and creative business owners to elevate their work, so that the people they are here to serve can find them.

Formerly the founder of STAGES, an alternative mental health charity for seven years, Katie is an advocate for Mental Health and Emotional Wellbeing, particularly since her own health was affected when she was ill-health retired due to disabilities at the Age of 48, with conditions brought about by trauma and a life-time of toxic relationships.

Katie loves blending science and spirituality together and collaborates with people on the same wavelength in her multi-author books. Most authors have stories of synchronicities that led to them writing in books with Katie.

Katie's aim is to bring these concepts and ideas to more people who are seeking ways to support their own mental, spiritual, emotional, and physical wellbeing.

Katie has a history of working in TV, Radio, and Theatre as an Actress and Singer, which she manifested into her life in her teens. Katie lives in a Northamptonshire Village in the UK, where she is a Mum to three adult children and "Nanny Katie" to her grandchildren. Katie has made it her life's work to educate people to find healthier solutions and break free from ancestral, toxic, and generational patterns of lack and trauma. Katie is passionate about raising consciousness and currently does this with her work as a Mentor, Coach, Podcaster, Author, Publisher, and through her songs and poetry.

If you would like to collaborate with Katie in one of her multi-author books or to write your own solo book, you can contact Katie below:

Website: https://www.soulfulvalley.com

Email: soulfulvalleypodcast@gmail.com

FB, Twitter, IG and LinkedIn @soulfulvalley

Podcast: https://apple.co/3BkJdkn

Katie's Amazon Author Profile:

ENTANGLED NO MORE

More books co-authored by Katie Carey Available on Amazon.

Evolving on Purpose: Mindful Ancestors Paving the Way for Future Generations
Intuitive: Knowing Her Truth
Soul Warrior: Accessing Realms Beyond the Veil

Made in the USA
Middletown, DE
27 October 2022

13642609R00190